Wageless Life

Forerunners: Ideas First

Short books of thought-in-process scholarship, where intense analysis, questioning, and speculation take the lead

FROM THE UNIVERSITY OF MINNESOTA PRESS

(Continued on page 132)

Wageless Life

A Manifesto for a Future
beyond Capitalism

Ian G. R. Shaw and
Marv Waterstone

University of Minnesota Press

MINNEAPOLIS

LONDON

Published by the University of Minnesota Press, 2019
111 Third Avenue South, Suite 290
Minneapolis, MN 55401–2520
http://www.upress.umn.edu

The University of Minnesota is an equal-opportunity educator and employer.

Contents

Introduction: The Coming Storm

A VAST TEMPEST is gathering on the horizon. You can feel the wind howling, see the darkness in the sky, and taste the electricity in the air. World capitalism is imploding—its destiny ever since Europeans began the great plunder of 1492. Billions of lives have been shipwrecked in the wake of capital's planetary assaults, each attack waged under different national banners. But now even those populations in the fortressed centers of the planet—the fabled "middle classes"—are being swept into the same catastrophe. The coming storm is not bound to the global South: its eye is lurching upwards. Signs abound in the streets and violences of everyday life. Soaring inequality, stagnation, oligarchic corruption, debt, and a simmering depression tear through the advanced economies. Once paired with Western democracy in a shotgun marriage, capitalism is now unhinged, naked, and angry. Eight men own the same wealth as half the world, and the richest one percent possess more than the planet's 99 percent.[1] Staggering but not surprising, this statistic evokes cynical shrugs: despondence but not despair. Where is the outrage? So pervasive is capitalism that our minds have been beaten into submission. A global Stockholm syndrome weighs heavily on the prisoners of capital's long war of attrition.

To be alive on planet Earth, spinning 93 million miles from the sun, is to be weighed down by capital and its discontents. Few escape its punishing gravity.

Capitalism is more than just an economic system: it is an existential conflict felt deep in our bones, our minds, and our ecosystems. For centuries the great war of enclosure has privatized soils,

1. Oxfam 2017.

seas, and airs—dispossessing billions of their lands, livelihoods, and dignity. In the colonial heartlands of the global North, a minority population were fattened. The looting of black and brown bodies, their ecologies, and their knowledges created a global inequality that defined modernity and still structures the world market. But the lines between the "haves" and the "have-nots" are bleeding. The violence that created wealth for a few is now directed at everyone. A vicious war of all against all defines twenty-first-century neoliberalism—an epoch that no longer abides the post–World War II welfare contracts between capital and labor. Since the 1970s, a neoliberal monster—a serpent with many heads—has devoured unions, institutions, and social safety nets, profaning all that is sacred and destroying all that is solid. Many of us have long seen this monster. But a storm is coming that will shake even this bloodthirsty Leviathan.

The old bulwarks against exploitation and outright extermination—the labor movement, and labor power in general—are increasingly ineffective. Capital now extracts billions in profit *without* a mass of workers or consumers. Upon the ashes of Fordist capitalism stand the citadels of finance capital, protected by a ring of borders and angry drones. In the heart of its empire, Wall Street and the City of London, algorithms make billions of dollars of trades in microseconds. And the slow march of the robot army with its weapons of mass automation threaten all sectors of employment. On the outside of this hypersecured enclosure—amongst the dirt and the debris—stand a worldless multitude, crying out into the storm. Planetary problems are everywhere declared. Some call it the Anthropocene, others the Capitalocene.[2] Many of the dire symptoms are the same: ubiquitous neo-imperial conflicts, volatile climate change, rising sea waters, plastic oceans, and a range of ecological disasters. But today something equally portentous looms for the human species. Capitalism, a system built on sys-

2. Moore 2017.

tematic expulsion, can no longer manage a booming outcast humanity. As David Harvey defines our desperate situation:

> Oligarchic capitalist class privilege and power are taking the world in a similar direction almost everywhere. Political power backed by intensifying surveillance, policing, and militarised violence is being used to attack the well-being of whole populations deemed expendable and disposable. We are daily witnessing the systematic dehumanisation of disposable people.[3]

We believe we are reaching a momentous conjuncture in capitalism's cruel history: a planet of "surplus" populations. Surplus, that is, to capitalism.[4] Billions now live outside of a shrinking economic order. The condition of wageless life befalls the globe. As Mike Davis describes, "This outcast proletariat—perhaps 1.5 billion people today, 2.5 billion by 2030—is the fastest-growing and most novel social class on the planet."[5] As he adds, "this is a mass of humanity structurally and biologically redundant to global accumulation and the corporate matrix." We live on a planet where billions of disposable lives dwell in the wastelands of a shrinking economic order. A planet where the bodies of refugees wash up on the shores of Europe or perish in the deserts of the U.S. southwest. While capitalism once "recycled" its outcast lives into productive workers—*if you were lucky*—now the unemployed are becoming permanently abandoned. These leftover lives, with no economic utility or social significance, constitute what Zygmunt Bauman calls a *disposable humanity,* "the waste products of globalization."[6] Unemployed workers in America's Rust Belt, or young people across Europe, now join the slums in the global South for "warehousing this century's surplus humanity."[7] And as the skies darken, our political leaders bury their heads.

3. Harvey 2014, 292.
4. Marx 1990.
5. Davis 2004, 11.
6. Bauman 2004, 66.
7. Davis 2006, 201.

Surplus populations rendered economically redundant are politically and socially intolerable to the ruling order. As Bauman warns, "we have not however arrived anywhere near to seeing clearly and grasping in full the far-reaching effects of the growing masses of 'wasted humans' on the political balance and social equilibrium of human planetary coexistence."[8] In the desperate slums, the violent ghettos, the rotten towers of social housing, and rusted industrial factories, we find so many ghosts. But so too is the reverse true: populations marked as politically redundant (such as refugees) are rendered economically intolerable. Not since the Second World War have there been more worldless persons on the planet: more than 68.5 million people were displaced in 2019.[9] Each refugee embodies a piece of the planetary crisis. Yet they are met at the doors of the better-off with disdain. Surplus populations—at least those with white skin—were once provided with incentives to be reintegrated into liberal democracy: typically, a pastoral power of economic rehabilitation. Increasingly, there is no such incentive to absorb—only to secure the gates between a shrinking set of "insiders" and a growing mass of "outsiders." The planet is now stuffed with outsiders: worldless multitudes denied basic human rights and dignity. Worldlessness is our shared existential condition.

Every system has a tipping point: a threshold that, if exceeded, becomes permanently destabilized. For Immanuel Wallerstein, "the modern world-system in which we are living cannot continue because it has moved too far from equilibrium, and no longer permits capitalists to accumulate endlessly. . . . We are consequently living in a structural crisis in which there is a struggle about the successor system."[10] In 2008, the worst depression since the 1930s failed to transform capitalism's destructive tendencies: the rich have become richer, and the poor poorer. So enormous is the

8. Bauman 2004, 70.
9. United Nations High Commissioner for Refugees, 2019.
10. Wallerstein 2013, 36.

gulf between the one percent and the 99 percent that its very existence has permanently altered capitalism. Every day, perverse inequities distort the legal system, the environment, our social institutions, politics, and our very human being. The system has, in other words, snapped beyond its ability to repair itself. It is extremely unlikely that we can return to a more "socially just" form of capitalism—a phenomenon so rare in human history that it only existed between 1945 and the late 1970s, and only for a handful of countries and populations. We are instead returning to the desperate conditions of nascent capitalism in the nineteenth century: mass dispossession, mass unemployment, mass inequality, mass corruption. Yet without the luxury of the poorhouses!

The present system prolongs its death like a zombie. You can smell its rot everywhere. "Before capitalism will go to hell," writes Wolfgang Streeck, "it will for the foreseeable future hang in limbo, dead or about to die from an overdose of itself but still very much around, as nobody will have the power to move its decaying body out of the way."[11] What is dying is capitalism as a system: a coherent, self-correcting machine with recognizable institutions, actors, and states. Of course, for most of the planet's population, capitalism never had a welfare state to counteract its excesses. The global South has long been the site of capital's most violent extremes and still endures conditions of unfreedom and slavery. As we argue later in this book, it is precisely these communities in the global South that may provide us with strategies and tactics for surviving *beyond* capital's flinching corpse. What does this *beyond* look like?

The death of capitalism weighs heavily on all of us. "Whether we acknowledge it or not, we are living amidst a struggle for the successor system,"[12] writes Wallerstein. Yet despite (or because of) these wretched conditions, new worlds are struggling to breathe. Many "alternative" visions remain retrograde or toxic. Galvanized

11. Streek 2017, 36.
12. Wallerstein 2013, 32.

white supremacists are exploiting the volatile mix of neoliberalism and racism to implant new, authoritarian regimes. And the solutions touted by so many economists recycle the same old nonsense: tax cuts, deregulation, privatization, "trickle-down!" Antonio Gramsci framed such a "crisis of authority" as follows:

> If the ruling class has lost its consensus, i.e. is no longer "leading" but only "dominant," exercising coercive force alone, this means precisely that the great masses have become detached from their traditional ideologies, and no longer believe what they used to believe previously, etc. The crisis consists precisely in the fact that the old is dying and the new cannot be born; in this interregnum a great variety of morbid symptoms appear.[13]

And yet, our dark interregnum may also be an opportunity to fundamentally reimagine what constitutes a good life and to build more dignified worlds. Even in the direst of conditions, however, we still cling to the world we have, rather than the world we want. Our landscapes, oceans, bodies, and minds are so colonized by what Mark Fisher terms "capitalist realism"[14] that its suffocating power can be difficult to discern. In fact, despite the myriad threats posed by late-stage capitalism, Fisher (echoing other analysts) declares that "it is easier to imagine the end of the world than to imagine the end of capitalism."[15] To that end, this book takes aim at this hegemonic "common sense" of our times: that the solution to capitalism is more capitalism. Legions of articles, speeches, and blog posts provide ample critiques of capitalism's many ills. But we see our task in this book as not only providing a diagnostic for our interregnum but also reenchanting our political imaginations. We write with passion about a postcapitalist politics centered on building what we will eventually term "alter-worlds." These are shared spaces of autonomous coexistence. Across these pages, we emphasize the importance of existential and spatial au-

13. Gramsci 1971, 556.
14. Fisher 2009.
15. Fisher 2009, 1.

tonomy for our health, freedom, dignity, and survival. Reclaim territory, reclaim existence: a new *Right to the World*.[16]

A planet of surplus populations is fundamentally a source of geographic injustice. Our future depends on building different worlds. We are, after all, spatial animals. Our sense of self is bound to the spaces that we inhabit. Space is the canvas of our being: we impress in the world our individuality, passing from the obscurity of inexistence to the security of coexistence. We are beings-in-the-world. But capitalism is world-denying. By dispossessing us of our land, robbing us of our livelihoods, and enclosing the spaces for us *to be,* capitalism generates an enormous loss within the flesh and bones of the world. It then monetizes this loss: selling it all back to us.[17] The planet becomes commodified. Since its inception, capitalism has been an existential *expulsion*: the accumulation of capital is mirrored by a profound loss of world and self. Liberal prescriptions for social justice that do not consider spatial autonomy and are oriented by the "worker" or a "universal basic income" are still caged within the machine. We must instead ask: who owns the earth? Who should own the earth?

All around us are the living, breathing commons: the great oceans, forests, mountains, rivers, schools, hospitals, libraries, parks, languages, knowledges, skills, and dreams that populate the enchanted mosaic of our co-being. Yet these spaces are endlessly enclosed by capital and its imperial stormtroopers. Undoing this accumulation by dispossession is vital.[18] Politics must take its bearings from lived experience, from being thrown in an enclosed planet. "Since capital requires the separation of the worker from the means of production and subsistence," writes Peter Linebaugh, "and since the most important such means is land, commoning must logically ground the answer to the ills of a class-riven soci-

16. Nevins 2017.
17. Ward and Swyngedouw 2018.
18. Harvey 2014.

ety."[19] The resistance has forgotten how to build, forgotten that it
has forgotten, and what's worse, has few resources left to engineer
alter-worlds. But try we must. We, the alienated, must dream more
boldly than ever before. Of new worlds, new modes of existence,
new socialities: a new *common sense* to replace the stagnant imaginations of today. Wageless life is a tragedy but also an opportunity.

And so, we write this book because we must. We see our role as
sentinels: ringing the bell to warn of the coming storm. We must
reeducate, reorganize, and reequip ourselves so that we are ready
for the long night. Our book proceeds forward like a spiral. We
sometimes go backward to understand our future. Other times
we explore the conditions of the present. But always we seek geographic justice. That is our compass in troubled times. Our main
contribution is to view human existence as fundamentally *pau-
perized* under capital. Many of us are *actual* paupers, living with
only the shirts on our back—but most of us are *virtual* paupers,[20]
teetering on the edge of disaster. Each of us is always becoming-
surplus to capital. That's because our worlds—our geographies,
our commons, our peoples—have been stolen. And we need to get
them back.

Our book has ten sections and a set of final thoughts. The next
section grapples with the contemporary discontents of capitalism. We focus on understanding neoliberalism, inequality, finance
capital, and the garrison state. In section 2, we analyze Karl Marx
and Friedrich Engels's writings on surplus populations. Our focus
is on the technological displacement of labor. This provides the
basis for understanding the dawn of "robot feudalism." Section
3 visits the "ground zero" of capitalism: the great war of enclosure in England. This robbery of the commons is a foundational
violence that remains vital to revisit. We also draw on the work

19. Linebaugh 2014, 110.
20. Marx 1973.

of Karl Polanyi to understand the deskilling of humanity's autonomous capacities and what Marx called the "virtual pauper." In section 4, we emphasize the existential conditions of capitalism. We explore Marx's important writings on alienation, and Hannah Arendt's philosophy of worldlessness. Both are important for understanding the link between capitalism and the human condition. In section 5, we explore the spaces of surplus lives: from the U.S. prison-industrial complex to the global slum. In section 6, we explore capitalism and slavery in the global South, drawing on Frantz Fanon's notion of the lumpenproletariat and Cedric Robinson's writings on racial capitalism.

The book then shifts to discuss a series of exit strategies. In section 7, we discuss various survival strategies in the global South. These provide lessons, skills, and toolkits for understanding postcapitalist worlds, including a discussion of the Zapatistas in Mexico. Their example is important for understanding territorial autonomy as a political goal. In section 8, we focus on the crucial importance of desire and the imagination as sites of political struggle against capitalism. This brings in key insights from Mark Fisher, Gilles Deleuze, and Félix Guattari. In section 9, we elaborate the essential links between justice and an autonomous production of space. We therefore explore Henri Lefebvre's work, particularly the notion of *autogestion*. We finish by presenting the notion of a *right to the world*. In section 10, we offer our main manifesto for building alter-worlds. These are spaces of postcapitalist commons animated by an entirely different cosmology. We articulate the types of work, subjectivities, and politics that enable their fruition. Our closing thoughts restate the importance of alienation as a central existential—and political—condition.

Capital's Morbid Symptoms

A New Dark Age

We live in a world sculpted by money but populated by the moneyless. The global North—the subject of this section—now finds itself riven with inequality, stagnation, debt, despotism, and corruption. And these social ills are mutually exacerbating. Economic growth, once a lever to *close* the gap between the rich and poor (especially between 1945 and the 1970s) is at historic lows in industrialized countries. Productivity gains have not led to an increase in wages. Instead, an extremely high rate of return on capital has created enormous inequality between those with and without capital. Such levels of income and wealth inequality are at rates not seen since the 1920s.[1] Inequality, in turn, dampens economic growth by reducing effective demand (i.e. both the desire and the means to purchase). And the response among the poorest has been to acquire huge levels of debt—benefiting, once again, those with capital. As Simon Hallsworth and John Lea write, "decades of slow growth . . . have decimated the old working class, eroded its power as a collective actor and at the same time flooded the ranks for the global surplus population."[2]

Neoliberal states have reacted to depressed economies by increasing the supply of money rather than redistributing wealth through progressive tax regimes. The result is that the middle class—the trophy of twentieth-century Fordism—is shrinking. Fast. "Life in a society of this kind," writes Streeck, "offers rich opportunities to oligarchs and warlords alike while imposing in-

1. Piketty 2014.
2. Hallsworth and Lea 2011, 144.

security on all others, in some ways like the long interregnum that began the fifth century CE and is now called the Dark Age."[3] The categorical imperative to *work!* is a cruel ethic for a world of unemployment and a reminder that this world was never created for human happiness. For all these reasons, it is amazing that capitalism has survived this long. Endless accumulation for accumulation's sake is an oppressive tautology. Motivating an entire society to work for products they don't need, in conditions they don't want, requires a range of brutal psychic apparatuses.[4]

Capitalism pivots on a range of destructive contradictions.[5] The most fundamental is the violent contradiction between the needs of capital and labor. Consider, by example, the technological displacement of labor: replacing humans with machines. This is a big structural weakness of capitalism—and is increasingly pronounced in an age of automation, artificial intelligence, and robots (explored later in the book). Automation is destroying the same middle-class jobs that were born in the rubble of manual industries. One outcome, if unchecked, would be a new class division between a handful of robot owners and *everybody else*. But this is just one of many contradictions. Consider the pervasive misery amongst workers and the unemployed. Or the toxic state of our ecosystems. Capitalism is located within the minds of depressed workers no less than in the plastic accumulating at the bottom of the oceans. Capital is a planetary disease: a war of profit against life on earth.

Many have predicted the fall of capitalism: Marx, Keynes, Polanyi, Luxemburg, Kondratieff. But here we are—still drowning in capitalism's morbid symptoms, still comfortably numb, still reeling. Organized opposition is at a historic low (which, ironically, always played an important role in propping up capitalism by restraining its excesses). This lack of alternatives persists despite

3. Streeck 2017, 36–37.
4. Graeber 2018.
5. Harvey 2014.

capitalism's multiple crises: global inflation in the 1970s, the explosion of public debt in the 1980s, private debt in 1990s, and the collapse of the banking (debt) system in 2008. Since its most recent shock, capitalism has entered a phase of deep indeterminacy. Yet the hold that capitalism has on our imaginations is so utterly resolute that the political response to a global financial meltdown was to print trillions of dollars out of thin air. Market fundamentalism simply piles misery and uncertainty upon itself. The result is that we have entered a lasting period of social and institutional entropy. Capitalism is dying from a thousand cuts. "A society in interregnum, in other words, would be a *de-institutionalized* or *under-institutionalized* society . . . and which for this very reason is essentially ungovernable," writes Streek.[6]

Capital's decline is neither singular nor momentous. *It is the slow rot of a zombie social formation.* And the rot is acutely felt in our bodies, minds, and landscapes of everyday life.[7] The real tragedy of capitalism's death is that no organized successor appears ready to take its place. Capital's death will be drawn out and painful. A neofeudal oligarchy could simply extract as much wealth out of the declining system as possible. The Dark Age we have already entered is a period of *desocialized capitalism,* moral decline (from new-fascist organizations to asset-stripping corporations), underinstitutionalized life, all sold by the false prophets of freedom. Token safety nets will no longer prevent a churning human catastrophe. Davis puts the situation bluntly: "The labour-power of a billion people has been expelled from the world system, and who can imagine any plausible scenario, under neoliberal auspices, that would reintegrate them as productive workers or mass consumers?"[8]

The capitalist world system no longer seeks to incorporate those it dispossesses. Expulsion is a planetary condition. "The past two

6. Streeck 2017, 14.
7. Hitchen 2016; Hitchen and Shaw 2019.
8. Davis, 2004, 27.

decades," writes Saskia Sassen, "have seen a sharp growth in the number of people, enterprises, and places expelled from the core social and economic orders of our time."[9] Unlike inequality, expulsion is a potentially irreversible capitalist pathology that tosses humans and nonhumans into the dump. Permanently. Examples of expulsion range from the expelling of the unemployed from government social welfare to ecological enclosure such as mining, which has "the power to transform natural environments into dead land and dead water, an expulsion of bits of life itself from the biosphere."[10] The problem is unprecedentedly acute, and the scale dramatic, far more so than the period of deindustrialization that hit advanced economies in the 1980s. From a record number of displaced peoples to the millions of bodies passing through the prison-industrial complex, to families warehoused in ghettos and slums, a trend is clear: *expulsion is epidemic*. What's worse, as capital's rot spreads, local expulsions are viewed as isolated events. Casualties of the new Dark Age are unable to see their shared plight.

Neoliberalism and Inequality

The neoliberal zombiescape we find ourselves in is not natural, normal, or inevitable. It was executed under a swift, highly coordinated class war, backed by wealthy elites, and installed in the thrones of power. Yet capitalism, in turn, has survived *only* on the basis that it is protected from its own excesses. In the twentieth century these protective measures were at their strongest in the global North. The Great Depression of the 1930s and the Second World War both produced fiscal and monetary policies that benefited (white, male) labor. Under a broadly Keynesian redistributive socioeconomic regime, European and American labor were at their most powerful. Capital, too, benefited from this grand bar-

9. Sassen 2014, 1.
10. Sassen 2014, 2.

gain, and this was always the conscious aim of figures like Keynes. By the 1970s, the great postwar settlement was under threat from waves of inflationary and debt crises. A reactionary right seized these discontents as a pretext to regain power and shift economic "common sense." By the 1980s their coup was orthodox policy in London and Washington, D.C. Who were these neoliberals?

The Mont Pelerin Society was founded in 1947 by Friedrich von Hayek—author of *Road to Serfdom* and *The Constitution of Liberty*—and Milton Friedman, who wrote the influential *Capitalism and Freedom*. Both figures were critical of collectivist state policy and instrumental in constructing the doctrine named neoliberalism. Although neoliberalism orbits around many theories, it typically refers to policies favorable to the sanctity of private property, "free" markets, and "free" trade—thereby disembedding capital from Keynesian checks and balances. Neoliberalism, of course, is not designed to spread wealth but is remarkably efficient at accumulating capital for the few. Neoliberalism was, and is, a class-restoration project.[11] The magical idea that wealth somehow "trickles down" from the rich was an attractive proposition to global elites. Not surprisingly, giving money to the rich only makes them richer—and leaves society unstable. But neoliberals worked hard to sell the snake oil.

A new "Washington Consensus" was quickly institutionalized in the 1980s under the administrations of Ronald Reagan and Margaret Thatcher. A key architect was Paul Volcker, then-Chairman of the U.S. Federal Reserve Bank (1979 to 1987), who engineered the abandonment of New Deal principles. His monetary policies favored quelling inflation no matter the costs—including the evisceration of organized labor. After raising interest rates to dampen inflation, Reaganites pursued supply-side (trickle-down) economics, supposedly to increase the amount of money the rich would redistribute downward. Top-rates of income and capital-gains tax were slashed.

11. Harvey 2005.

Finally, Washington neoliberals began to deregulate the financial sector. The result of this "Volcker Shock" was soaring inequality, falling real wages, sluggish growth, periodic financial crashes, and successive attacks against the welfare state.

Welfare state capitalism (circa 1945 to 1970s) is one of the few times in history that economic growth and social democracy have peacefully coexisted in the global North. Far more common is the brutal form of capitalism born in the industrial revolution and exhumed by neoliberal ideology. The effects of the neoliberal coup in the 1980s are still present and have spread far beyond the United States and the United Kingdom. As a result, global neoliberalism now creates planetary problems. The outsourcing of labor to countries such as China—with inadequate labor protections—has placed an incredible strain on labor in the global North, even as workers have enjoyed incredible (though largely debt-financed) purchasing power as consumers. But absent an international wealth tax,[12] it is local states that now clean up the global mess. Capitalist markets are no longer contained within states—instead, states are located within capitalist markets. All these challenges seem insurmountable. But an important lesson from the ascent of neoliberalism was how quickly common sense can, and does, change.

Neoliberalism continues to breed enormous inequality across the globe. Poverty is still very high, despite some important progress in the twentieth century. Around a billion people live below the "poverty line" of $1.90 per day—although this "official" figure set by the World Bank is punitively low. A more meaningful measurement, such as the "ethical poverty line," places 4.2 billion in poverty.[13] In Europe, *chronic* poverty is a persistent problem.[14] The share of unemployed people seeking work for over twelve months

12. Piketty 2014.
13. Hickel 2015.
14. The progress is difficult to document and to assess. Both the metric itself and the data to substantiate its value are changeable and notoriously arduous to obtain.

was approximately 50 percent in 2016. And more than two-thirds of this group (or 6 million) were unemployed for *over* two years.[15] In Sub-Saharan Africa, nearly two thirds of workers live in extreme or working poverty. Underscoring this poverty, the top one percent of the global population now owns more wealth than the rest of the planet. In the United States, the 0.1 percent now own as much wealth as the bottom 90 percent.[16]

This inequality has sustained a "super rich" class of oligarchs. These men—who prop up a violent patriarchal order—either rule directly, as with Russian barons, or purchase their political legitimacy by influencing the electoral process, as in the United States.[17] The net result is an international oligarchy of wealthy capitalists who shift their capital across borders and are disembedded from their "host" country and the demands of ordinary people. And while these men, together with their gigantic multinational corporations, do not necessarily "conspire" together as a conscious unit, each recognizes (mistakenly, in the long run) the benefits of the neoliberal order. Accumulation for accumulation's sake—the rest be damned—is sacrosanct orthodoxy for the one percent. The result is that extreme poverty and extreme wealth sit side-by-side. What Davis calls a "drastic diminution of the intersections between the lives of the rich and the poor"[18] is a form of social apartheid that exists between nations and streets. Everywhere the world is splintering.

Finance Capital and Debt

Within the new Dark Age, it is possible, in the short term, for capital accumulation to continue taking place without workers or consumers.[19] We see this in headlines about a "jobless" economic recovery,

---

15. International Labour Office 2017, 1.
16. Monaghan 2014.
17. Streeck 2017, 29.
18. Davis 2006, 119.
19. Lapavitsas 2013.

or an increase in GDP without a rise in median income. This is due to the overwhelming role finance capital plays in the global North. The stagnation of the world economy in the late 1970s led the capitalist class to find a new, more speculative—*more predatory*—source of accumulation. Finance capital is now the principal lever of accumulation for the ultra-rich. Within a matter of decades, derivatives and futures markets have completely overshadowed the sphere of production. The Volcker shock and neoliberal assault set in motion the perilous deregulation of the banking industry that underwrote the 2008 economic crisis (and like Japan in 1990, the consequences of the crash will be felt for decades). Even disaster is profitable for Wall Street and the City of London—its honorable vultures make billions by betting *against* growth and recovery. But in no way is printing money, trading derivatives, and betting on disaster sustainable for the long term. The destructive crises of capital will simply increase in scale and frequency.

Why is this source of instability and social violence not immediately stopped? The short answer is that financialization has utterly coopted democracy.[20] Finance capital is so powerful it has enthralled the pockets and minds of politicians (both directly and indirectly). National governments and their central banks will literally print money out of thin air to keep the finance sector afloat. In the decade after the 2008 crisis, the U.S. Federal Reserve has purchased bonds worth $3.7 trillion. Between March 2009 and July 2012, the Bank of England purchased government securities worth £375 million. And between 2009 to 2016, the European Central Bank purchased €1.1 trillion.[21] This so-called quantitative easing was executed at the same time government austerity policies slashed social welfare. The result was a regressive transfer of wealth from the poorest to the richest. And the noble debt economy kicked in to become a permanent source of rent on the indebted masses.

20. Blakeley 2019.
21. Venn 2018, 36.

Financialization creates—and feeds on—staggering levels of public and private debt. Since neoliberal reform stagnated real wages, credit cards have become a means of survival for those on the edge of financial ruin. In the United States, politicians first relaxed usury laws in the 1970s, paving the way for the billion-dollar credit industries of today. Unsecured credit has soared for the underemployed and unemployed (the so-called subprime market). In the United States the most exploited borrowers are typically African Americans, Latinos, and single women. As Susanne Soederberg writes, "the credit card industry has also continually sought to expand its debtor base by tapping into the unbanked and underbanked sectors of the surplus population."[22] Financing capital's problems with capital's solutions is a wonderfully lucrative system. All of this is regulated by a neoliberal state that aims to police an indebted society and protect the order of indebtedness. Put bluntly, neoliberal states do not condense the will of a popular sovereignty: they secure economic policies favorable to a financial elite.[23]

The Garrison State

The state is not a single "thing" but an assemblage of institutions, often with divergent logics. It has repressive and violent institutions, such as the police and the military, but also provides services that are a lifeline to the poor. It is a tragedy to see underfunded public-sector workers—such as teachers—battling to make the lives of deprived children slightly more tolerable. However much an overdetermined constellation, the state must nonetheless manage the pronounced social entropy of capitalism. And here it encounters a big contradiction: the mismatch between the state's spatial extent and authority, and the unrestricted spatial extent of capitalism.[24] This produces innumerable problems (consider la-

22. Soederberg 2013, 503.
23. Smith 2011.
24. Harvey 2003.

bor offshoring, tax avoidance, economic crises, or climate change). The welfare state is *not* dead, but it is being picked apart systematically by the ruling class. "Elites" continue to hound politicians to restore their class power, regulate deregulation, enact authoritarian business climates, and enclose the remaining commons. Despite the 2008 economic crisis—a *result* of neoliberal reform— much of austerity-hit Europe and North America has doubled-down on neoliberal policies. More tax cuts, more privatization, more welfare cuts.

But here we find another contradiction: with lower tax incomes, neoliberal states can no longer provide their citizens with economic security. Their own *legitimacy* under such failure becomes a key source of anxiety. As a result, many states have begun to recast security away from economic and political rights and toward a theater of existential danger. Authoritarianism has increasingly become a solution to crises of state legitimacy. As Bauman describes it, "A new popular demand for a strong state power capable of resuscitating the fading hopes of protection against a confinement to waste."[25] State legitimacy is oriented by capturing social unrest and directing it toward surplus populations, or so-called dangerous others. This new state formation is what Hallsworth and Lea call a security state.[26] "It aims not at the incorporation of all social classes into the State through nationalist unity but at the management of social fragmentation and the 'advanced marginality' of a growing global surplus population rendered 'structurally irrelevant' to capital accumulation."[27] As they add, forms of "preemptive criminalization, accompanied by CCTV and intrusive surveillance, are used to drive away the surplus population who are now defined as security risks."[28]

Henry Giroux, in a similar vein, describes the rise of the "garrison state." This intensifies neoliberal logics and technologies of con-

25. Bauman 2004, 91.
26. Hallsworth and Lea 2011.
27. Hallsworth and Lea 2011, 142.
28. Hallsworth and Lea 2011, 145.

trol. As Giroux writes, it "increasingly protects corporate interests while stepping up the level of repression and militarization on the domestic front."[29] The garrison state organizes the warehousing of the destitute in prisons,[30] polices and militarizes everyday life,[31] and materializes dangerous forms of necropolitics.[32] Crucially, the garrison state proffers its legitimacy by the manufacturing of a (racialized) enemy population: immigrants, terrorists, criminals, and the poor. Each of these populations—disciplined by mass surveillance, war, torture, drone executions, prisons, and refugee camps—are continuously growing. The garrison state must fortify capitalism's shrinking inside from a growing outside. Unlike the welfare state's attempt at inclusion and integration, garrison states are *policing disintegration*—excluding "outsiders" from the socioeconomic order. The most depressing but obvious conclusion is that the welfare state was a blip in capital's long war of enclosure.

29. Giroux 2002, 142.
30. Gilmore 2007; Wacquant 2009.
31. Wall 2016.
32. Mbembe 2003.

Surplus Populations

Victorian Waste

Surplus populations were manufactured at unprecedented rates during the industrial revolution. The factories were spewing out textiles, smoke, slag, and a disposable humanity. Between 1760 and 1840 the industrial revolution ripped through England. But it did not bring uniform wealth to the great cities. Instead, the proliferating mills brought wretched conditions, a decline in real wages, mass deskilling and dispossession, unemployment, and social unrest to millions of people. Friedrich Engels wrote extensively about the abhorrent environments of England's booming surplus population: the "reserve army" begging on streets and scrambling for survival.

> This reserve army, which embraces an immense multitude during the crisis and a large number during the period which may be regarded as the average between the highest prosperity and the crisis, is the "surplus population" of England, which keeps body and soul together by begging, stealing, street-sweeping, collecting manure, pushing hand-carts, driving donkeys, peddling, or performing occasional small jobs. In every great town a multitude of such people may be found.[1]

Crucially, Engels and Marx did not view this growing surplus population as separate from the production of industrialized workers. As Marx argues, "it is capitalistic accumulation itself that constantly produces, and produces in the direct ratio of its own energy and extent, a relatively redundant population of labourers, *i.e.*, a population of greater extent than suffices for the average needs

---

1. Engels 2009, 96–97.

of the self-expansion of capital, and therefore a surplus popula-tion."[2] Capital, in short, always produces, and benefits from, sur-plus masses. The more surplus workers it produces, the more that commodity—labor power—is devalued.

The technological displacement of labor—replacing humans with machines—was a central contradiction of the industrial revolu-tion. It remains so. As capitalist development proceeds, competi-tion drives capitalists to invest in constant capital (the technical means of production) rather than variable capital (living labor). Machines, wherever possible, replace the expensive human body. Consequently, fewer and lesser-skilled workers are required, even as their productivity rises. For Marx, "the higher the productivity of labor, the greater is the pressure of the workers on the means of employment, the more precarious therefore becomes the condition for their existence, namely the sale of their own labor-power for the increase of alien wealth."[3] Precarity is the common denominator of capitalism and rises in relation to accumulation. As Marx ex-plains, "The labouring population therefore produces, along with the accumulation of capital produced by it, the means by which it itself is made relatively superfluous, is turned into a relative surplus population; and it does this to an always increasing extent."[4]

Marx subdivides the surplus population into three distinct stra-ta: floating, latent, and stagnant. The *floating* population consists of proletarianized workers who cycle in and out of work. In con-temporary terms, this is roughly equivalent to the "unemployed" of government statistics. The floating population is sensitive to fluctuations in the production process, outsourcing, and long-term economic trends. These workers bounce between short-term jobs, zero-hour contracts, and other forms of induced precarity. This now constitutes *most* work in the global North, and few manage to escape this destiny. The *latent* surplus population is created when

2. Marx 1990, 782.
3. Marx 1990, 798.
4. Marx 1990, 783.

"capitalist production takes possession of agriculture"[5] and reduces labor-demand in rural areas. This land enclosure is still present in rural areas of China, Mexico, and India, and even small U.S. family farms, where production is concentrated into gigantic agribusinesses. As Harvey observes, "whereas the floating population is roughly confined to the areas of capitalist organization, the latent reserve has very different geographical spread. It is potentially available everywhere, and the geopolitics of access to it through imperialist and colonial practices can play a very significant role."[6]

The final population, the *stagnant* group, "forms a part of the active labour army, but with extremely irregular employment. Hence it offers capital an inexhaustible reservoir of disposable labour power."[7] This stratum has the weakest connection to waged work and is chronically unemployed. And at its lowest ranks lies "the sphere of pauperism," including "vagabonds, criminals, prostitutes, in short the actual lumpenproletariat." The conditions of the stagnant population are the most wretched. The stagnant population has little, if any, hope of ever returning to (or entering) waged life. Whether stagnant, floating, or latent, the surplus population weakens and depresses the conditions of all workers, and thus executes a vital function for capital. But with fewer waged workers and more surplus populations, who will buy capital's bountiful carnival of products? Herein lies the problem of effective demand. Workers are simultaneously consumers. With a falling number of workers-as-*consumers,* capitalism struggles to sell its commodities. This has been temporarily "fixed" with an explosion in debt. But this structural contradiction remains a source of volatility, with a growing mass of humanity for whom capitalism has no need.

5. Marx 1990, 795.
6. Harvey 2010, 279.
7. Marx 1990, 796.

Outcast Lives

Our era is defined as one in which surplus populations no longer provide a residual function for capitalism (i.e., wage depression or a reserve army of labor). One of the characteristics that distinguished the floating strata of the surplus population—the unemployed—was its recyclability into and out of the labor force. What has changed, Bauman argues, is that recyclability has now, in many cases, turned into *disposability*. That is, for many workers, being thrown out of the labor force is no longer a temporary condition: they have become eternally redundant and thus disposable. What Bauman calls "human waste," or "wasted humans," are the products of economic progress, which devalues, degrades, and destroys all livelihoods incommensurate with capital. Surplus populations are the "unintended and unplanned 'collateral causalities' of economic progress"[8]— although, as Marx argued, these causalities are entirely predictable, as reinvestment switches from variable to constant capital. The manufacture of wasted humans appears as a technical process, but it is a crushing form of social violence.

Millions of outcast lives have been declared redundant. The living dead. "'Redundancy' shares its semantic space with 'rejects,' 'wastrels,' 'garbage,' 'refuse'—with *waste*. The destination of the *un*employed, of the 'reserve army of labour,' was to be called back into active service. The destination of waste is the waste-yard, the rubbish heap."[9] To be declared redundant, writes Bauman, "means to have been disposed of *because of being disposable*—just like the empty and non-refundable plastic bottle or once-used syringe, an unattractive commodity with no buyers."[10] This is important to understand. Disposal is an *act* enabled by the *condition of disposability*. In capital's eyes, humans are always-already disposable (or becoming-surplus) and can be replaced at any time. In

8. Bauman 2004, 39.
9. Bauman 2004, 12.
10. Bauman 2004, 12.

turn, capital's moral industry justifies and demonizes its wasted lives. This ideological attack insists "the superfluous are not just an alien body, but a cancerous growth gnawing at the healthy tissues of society and sworn enemies of 'our way of life' and 'what we stand for.'"[11] Surplus populations become enemies of the people.

Surplus populations were once exported to the "New World" under European colonialism (or, under other circumstances, to any available "frontier"): dispossessing the indigenous of their lands. But that option is no longer a possibility. World capitalism has seeped into nearly every pore of the planet, reducing the outlets for its wasted lives. There are few outsides—or dumping grounds—left. In fact, the opposite geographic flow now obtains: capital's discontents in the global South, structured by centuries of imperial conquest, are now returning home. States are scrambling to produce local solutions to global problems, on a planet *full* of surplus populations. For Bauman, "To cut the long story short: the new fullness of the planet means, essentially, *an acute crisis of the human waste disposal industry*. While the production of human waste goes on unabated and rises to new heights, the planet is fast running short of refuse dumps and the tools of waste recycling."[12] Instead, the social dumps emerge at the heart of the colonies: from urban ghettos to opioid- or meth-afflicted rural towns. Beyond the reservoirs of dead industrial labor are the oceans of refugees flowing to the metropole. The modern refugee crisis embodies the "the flotsam and jetsam of the planetary tides of human waste."[13]

Refugees are the epitome of human waste, "with no useful function to play in the land of their arrival."[14] By 2019, the number of people forcibly displaced from their homes across the globe was 68.5 million—a rate of 44,000 every day (fueled in large measure by conflicts such as those in the Democratic Republic of Congo,

11. Bauman 2004, 41.
12. Bauman 2004, 6.
13. Bauman 2004, 57.
14. Bauman 2004, 77.

Myanmar, Venezuela, and Syria). This means that the world's displaced population now exceeds that of the United Kingdom.[15] Fifty-two percent of all refugees are children. Indeed, 1 in every 110 people on earth is now an asylum seeker, internally displaced, or a refugee. In the Mediterranean region, hundreds of thousands of people—many of them Syrian refugees—have crossed its seas. Since 2014, more than 17,000 people have died (or gone missing) in such attempted crossings, the majority on their way to Italy or Greece. European states have often reacted with either violent action or violent *apathy*. As Bauman writes, "Forced to depend for their survival on the people on whose doors they knock, refugees are in a way thrown outside the realm of 'humanity,' as far as it is meant to confer the rights they aren't afforded. And there are millions upon millions of such people inhabiting our shared planet."[16]

Robot Feudalism

A big concern for the future of human redundancy is robotization and automation. The age of robots confronts us with profound questions about the nature of humanity.[17] "Two specters are haunting Earth in the twenty-first century: the specters of ecological catastrophe and automation,"[18] writes Peter Frase. And we would add a third: the intersection of both with militarism. In any case, the interrelated processes of computerization, automation, and robotization are producing social shocks like the industrial revolution did, centered around economic growth without increased wages. The *exponential* rather than linear growth in microchip processing means that robotization is progressing at a faster rate than any time since its invention. As Paul Krugman wrote, "we could be looking at a society that grows ever richer,

15. United Nations High Commissioner for Refugees 2019.
16. Evans and Bauman 2016.
17. Nast 2015.
18. Frase 2016, 10.

but in which all the gains in wealth accrue to whoever owns the robots."[19] Robots are revolutionizing—that is, *destroying*—the socioeconomic order. Marx famously wrote, "The hand-mill gives you society with the feudal lord; the steam-mill, society with the industrial capitalist."[20] What society do robots disclose? Feudalism or communism? Fascism or socialism? We stand on the precipice between a peaceful coexistence with robots or a system of brutal oppression. The conditions for violence and peace hang together. For Harvey,

> The paradox is that automation and artificial intelligence now provide us with abundant means to achieve the Marxian dream of freedom beyond the realm of necessity at the same time as the laws of capital's political economy put this freedom further and further out of reach.[21]

Robotic capital exacerbates existing wealth inequalities. Labor's contemporary share of national income now stands at a historic low. A big risk is that wealth (capital) and work (labor) further decouple to create a *jobless future*. As Andy Merrifield warns, "living labour is a species en route to extinction."[22] Over the past two decades, the distribution of income in nearly all advanced economies has shifted toward capital. For example, between 1990 and 2009, the share of national income in wages, salaries, and benefits declined in twenty-six of thirty OECD countries.[23] As Thomas Piketty observes, "There is little evidence that labor's share in national income has increased significantly in a very long time: 'nonhuman' capital seems almost as indispensable in the twenty-first century as it was in the eighteenth or nineteenth, and there is no reason why it may not become even more so."[24] Since the

19. Krugman 2012.
20. Marx 1999, chapter 2.
21. Harvey 2014, 208.
22. Merrifield 2013, 24.
23. Freeman 2015, 4–5.
24. Piketty 2014, 22.

early 1980s—when robotization and automation emerged—U.S. productivity has soared 65 percent, but for the top 80 percent of American workers, wages only grew 8 percent. The top one percent, conversely, increased their income by 154 percent.[25]

In the United States and United Kingdom, some economists predict that in the next few decades, half of all current jobs could be replaced.[26] Robots have already displaced human labor in factory floors since the 1970s. But advances in microchip processing are creating automatic systems capable of cognitive-intensive tasks. Skilled middle-class jobs, such as accountancy and the legal professions, are at risk no less than manufacturing jobs. This would lead to enormous pressure on labor. "If robots take the good jobs at high pay and humans get the low-pay leftovers, the living standards of persons dependent on labor income will fall."[27] Robotic-induced labor displacement, across all sectors of the economy, thus presents a *terminal* structural crisis by failing to provide alternative livelihoods. For Randall Collins, "New jobs are created, but they do not match the number of jobs eliminated, nor do they replace lost income."[28] For this reason, Collins adds, robotization "will bring capitalism to an end within the next thirty to fifty years."[29] And the political fallout is only coming into focus: research by Frey, Berger, and Chen shows a strong relationship between robotic unemployment and voting for Donald Trump in 2016.[30]

The risk of a robotic capitalism is a huge structural imbalance between the owners of robots and everybody else—already the situation with finance capital. "The real threat of the future," writes Collins, "is not some Frankensteinian revolt of the robots, but the last stage of technological displacement of labor on behalf of a

25. Frey, Berger, and Chen 2018, 425.
26. Frey and Osborne 2013.
27. Freeman 2015, 3.
28. Collins 2013, 40–41.
29. Collins, 37.
30. Frey, Berger, and Chen 2018.

tiny capitalist class of robot wonders."[31] The rich have no incentive to give up their power. "To the extent that the rich are able to maintain their power," writes Peter Frase, "we will live in a world where they enjoy the benefits of automated production, while the rest of us pay the costs of ecological destruction—if we can survive at all."[32] *Robotic feudalism* is thus a system in which the robotic means of production are owned by an extremely small elite. The rest of humanity fights for the scraps, building robots, repairing robots, and fighting robots.

In this dystopic robo-feudalism, a policy of "neo-exterminism" might be enacted. After all, as Bauman warns, "we can hardly visualize in advance the social settings that may define 'redundancy' and shape the human-waste disposal mechanisms of the future."[33] Those rendered obsolete by the robot are little more that potential saboteurs. Nuisances. Accordingly, as Frase warns:

A world where the ruling class no longer depends on the exploitation of working class labor is a world where the poor are merely a danger and an inconvenience. Policing and repressing them ultimately seem more trouble than can be justified. This is where the thrust toward "the extermination of multitudes" originates. Its ultimate endpoint is literally the extermination of the poor, so that the rabble can finally be brushed aside once and for all, leaving the rich to live in peace and quiet in their Elysium.[34]

When billions of humans are rendered surplus, and when robots are able to perform their own war of annihilation, "a final solution lurks: the genocidal war of the rich against the poor. . . . An exterminist society can automate and mechanize the process of suppression and extermination, allowing the rulers and their minions to distance themselves from the consequences of their actions."[35]

31. Collins 2013, 67.
32. Frase 2016, 30–31.
33. Bauman 2004, 42.
34. Frase 2013, 102.
35. Frase 2013, 107.

We *can* avoid robot feudalism. Much depends on the ownership of the means of production. Freeman advocates people own stocks in the robots that replace them, otherwise, "workers will become serfs working on behalf of the robots' overlords."[36] Likewise, Frase writes, "Who benefits from automation, and who loses, is ultimately a consequence not of the robots themselves, but of who owns them."[37] But it is difficult to imagine how owners of capital will concede anything. Surplus populations will never be safe unless they own the means of production themselves—and return to the commons stolen from beneath their feet.

36. Freeman 2015, 1.
37. Frase 2016, 25.

Ground Zero

CAPITALISM IS an oppressive spatial order that throws people off the land, robs them of their livelihood, and denies their unique calendar with the earth. Doreen Massey defines space "as the sphere in which distinct trajectories coexist; as the sphere therefore of coexisting heterogeneity."[1] Space is made up of many "stories-so-far." This recognizes that there isn't one space, but multiple. Capital's production of space, conversely, is one of a *universal surface* and a *universal time*. It insists that everyone and everything exists within an omnipresent "now." The trajectories of other cultures are denied their space-times, their calendars, their stories-so-far. Capitalist space is designed to be appropriated, chopped up, bordered, policed, erased, and sold. Capitalist time collapses the rich multiplicity of earth's cultures into a linear arc of progress: you exist either now or you are "stuck in the past." Rendering the planet worldless, stripping the earth of its singular time-spaces, ecologies, animal kingdoms, habitats, homes, social milieus, and cosmologies, defines capitalism's great war of enclosure—what Boaventura de Sousa Santos calls "epistemicide."[2]

Primitive Accumulation

For centuries, a long war of enclosure has generated immense misery by forcing all livelihoods into the singular orbit of capitalism.[3] The dawn of capitalism, writes Marx, was brutal, "dripping from

1. Massey 2005, 9.
2. Santos 2014.
3. Shaw 2016; 2017.

head to foot, from every pore, with blood and dirt."[4] An important starting point for capital was the woman's body—which was rapidly enclosed under patriarchal relations of private poverty. Indeed, capitalism has long been a hypermasculinist project that has erased—or else contained—the maternal. As Engels observed, women were the *first* form of private poverty.[5] For Heidi Nast, "Through private property, the maternal body, as the progenitor of *all* territorialized labor and value, was subsumed into abstractions of personal ownership."[6] Recent anxieties over the collapse of paternal rule—itself materialized in industrial machinery, or what Nast calls "the machine"[7]—are everywhere, including the hypermasculinity of authoritarian rulers and the global spread of an authoritarian, and hypersexed, far right. Capital, race, and sexuality share a complex geohistory.

Marx termed the "original sin" of capitalism primitive accumulation, or "the historical process of divorcing the producer from the means of production." We are thus *free* in a double sense according to Marx, "as a free individual he can dispose of his labour power as his own commodity, and that on the other hand, he has no other commodity for sale."[8] Marx argued forcefully for the inaugural *pauperization* of humanity as a precondition of capitalism. Swept off the land, denied their autonomy, the destiny for millions was the factory gates or the poorhouse. Crucially, then, primitive accumulation never held a guarantee: it doesn't *necessarily* produce a waged job for the dispossessed peasant, artisan, or commoner. There is no "social contract," only the forced imposition of the capitalist world order. Little wonder that Marx called primitive accumulation a "ruthless terrorism."

> The spoliation of the Church's property, the fraudulent alienation of the state domains, the theft of common lands, the usurpation of

4. Marx 1990, 926.
5. Engels 1972.
6. Nast 2017.
7. Nast 2015.
8. Marx 1990, 272.

feudal and clan property and its transformation into modern private property under circumstances of ruthless terrorism, all these things were just so many idyllic methods of primitive accumulation. They conquered for capitalist agriculture, incorporated the soil into capital, and created for the urban industries the necessary supplies of free and rightless proletarians.[9]

Marx's reference here was the English enclosure movement, which placed a huge existential burden on humanity. But this ruthless terrorism encompassed the other great dispossessions of modernity: the seizure of indigenous American lands under the cover of *terra nullius,* or the robbery of millions of African bodies. As he elsewhere writes, "The discovery of gold and silver in America, the extirpation, enslavement, and entombment in mines of the aboriginal population of that continent, the beginnings of the conquest and plunder of India, and the conversion of Africa into a preserve for the commercial hunting of blackskins, are all things which characterize the dawn of the era of capitalist production."[10]

Capitalism grew with, and because of, colonialism—its trails of tears spiral everywhere, and its ghosts haunt the planet. Modernity is built on imperial loot, and between 1750 and 1850 a liberal political economy became the dominant mode of globalization. Of course, primitive accumulation never stopped. This process of violent extraction and enclosure still operates today in unequal trade agreements, intellectual property rights and patents, new land enclosures and expulsions, and the commodification of everyday life. What Harvey calls accumulation by dispossession is the "dark matter" of political economy: the unseen processes of everyday life that commodify everything and everyone.[11] Capitalism's long war of enclosure places the planet *inside* its universal matrix of time, space, and exchange.

9. Marx 1990, 895.
10. Marx 1990, 915.
11. Harvey 2014.

The Enclosure of the English Commons

The enclosure of the English commons was a war of capital against the commons: the privatization of shared spaces of agriculture, husbandry, and being-together. As E. P. Thompson famously wrote, "Enclosure (when all the sophistications are allowed for) was a plain enough case of class robbery, played according to fair rules of property and law laid down by a parliament of property-owners and lawyers."[12] The enclosure of the commons was a war of existence fought over the ownership of the soil. For Karl Polanyi, "Enclosures have been appropriately called a revolution of the rich against the poor."[13] Enclosure converted open fields into closed property, and transformed autonomous communities into precarious wage laborers, under a brutal and relentless deworlding. "The 'English enclosure movement,'" writes Peter Linebaugh, "has belonged to that series of concrete universals—like the slave trade, the witch burnings, the Irish famine, or the genocide of Native Americans—that has defined the crime of modernism."[14]

Commoning is primary to human life: the commons are shared spaces of social coexistence. Life before capitalism was, of course, miserable for many—and often brutal (we discuss the racist foundations of European capitalism and slavery in section 6, "The Wretched of the Earth"). But there was certainly a different conception and use of space. The open-field agricultural system in England, together with indigenous practices across the world, practiced different cosmologies, different time-spaces, to the capitalist projection that now wraps and warps the planet. Peasants, commoners, serfs, smallholders, artisans, cottagers, all shared part of their livelihoods *with* the land, in looping ecologies that defy the labor-resource dualisms of contemporary capital. Survival, although fragile, did not simply depend on miserable wages or cruel

12. Thompson 1963, 238.
13. Polanyi 2001, 37.
14. Linebaugh 2014, 142.

working hours but on an ability to autonomously grow, share, and cooperate. Economies were not oriented *by* the market but were often tied to local spaces of reciprocity and exchange. Life was embedded in land, social practices, and cultural conventions. All were obstacles to the divine progress of capital.

Commoners were a group that included English peasants, artisans, cottagers, and smallholders.[15] They worked in open-fields and across England's commons: lands that were often attached to manors (such as "wastes") but were not individually held "properties." Instead, commons were collective spaces governed by custom and common law, and were vital for shared pasture, berrying, gleaning, gathering fuel, tending sheep, cutting peat, raising chickens, and so on. Even if commoners did not own the land, it was their right to occupy it, work it, and share in its fruits. Commoners were the "human fauna" of the land, living intimately *with* its geography.[16] As Neeson puts it, in a wonderful turn of phrase, "Landless commoners lived off the land rather than on it."[17] Commoners did not simply reside *on* the land, they were folded into its rich ecological spheres: existing *with* plants, rivers, nuts, berries, rabbits, pathways, bridges, fields, skylarks, rains. How many of us can say the same today? For billions of us, we have been made surplus to the land we walk on—our organic existence is alienated by capitalist property relationships.

The enclosure of the commons was a slow but violent process between the fifteenth and nineteenth centuries. Common land was privatized, sold off, chopped up, bordered, policed. And this production of capitalist space was underwritten by ideals of progress, including John Locke's philosophy of economic improvement and private property. Enclosure ruptured the traditional village customs and rights, "and the social violence of enclosure consisted precisely in the drastic, total imposition upon the vil-

15. Neeson 1993, 12.
16. Neeson 1993, 179.
17. Neeson 1993, 66.

lage of capitalist property-definitions."[18] Enclosure was a *loss of world*: a loss of mutuality and reciprocity—both with human and nonhuman neighbors. Between 1604 and 1914, more than 5,200 Acts of Parliamentary enclosure were enacted.[19] The big wave of enclosures started in the mid-eighteenth century. Between 1750 and 1820, more than 20 percent of England was enclosed by Act of Parliament, representing about 30 percent of agricultural land.[20] The publication of the 1872 Return of Owners of Land (or new Domesday Book) revealed that 0.6 percent of the population owned 98.5 percent of agricultural land.[21]

Despite noble defenses from commoners, the enclosure movement successfully created a landless surplus population, shipwrecked in the ruins of the ancient common economy. A deworlded humanity was now utterly dependent on the system responsible for its violent dispossession. As Polanyi summarizes, "the country folk had been dehumanized into slum dwellers; the family was on the road to perdition; and large parts of the country were rapidly disappearing under the slack and scrap heaps vomited forth from the 'satanic mills.'"[22] Enclosure was a psycho-social shock. For Thompson, "The loss of the commons entailed, for the poor, a radical sense of displacement."[23] The new psychogeographies of modernity were *enclosed*: a closed *architecture* and *anthropology*. Or as Linebaugh writes, "The world was being enclosed, life was being closed off, people shut in."[24] Commoners and common land were ubiquitous until the dawn of capitalism. This is important to recognize. If we fail to see this, England, and by extension, the precolonial world, is retroactively produced as a *terra nullius* of "proto-proletariats" awaiting capitalism. There is nothing more

18. Thompson 1963, 238.
19. UK Parliament 2016.
20. Neeson 1993, 329.
21. Fairlie 2009.
22. Polanyi 2001, 41.
23. Thompson 1963, 239.
24. Linebaugh 2014, 80.

toxic to the imagination. Before we were wageless and landless, many of us had the earth's commonwealth closer to our fingertips.

Disembedding the World

Our beautiful, tragic, journey on this planet was never defined by individual survivalism; it was possible only because of reciprocity, redistribution, and existential autonomy. Our branding as *Homo economicus* is a recent invention. The rise of the capitalist market economy is what Polanyi terms a *great transformation*.[25] Unlike other social revolutions, the capitalist revolution established an entirely market-based economy: a self-regulating system of markets, in which price determines everything else. The multidimensional ecologies of human activity are noise to the wants and needs of capitalist accumulation (at least until they can be colonized by the logic of the market).

All societies have possessed some form of economy, but no economy existed that was in principle *controlled* by the market system. Prior to market capitalism, human economies were *embedded* in society and played a subordinate role to custom, religion, law, and other social relations. The maintenance of reciprocal ties was crucial, and there was social pressure to eliminate economic self-interest. Human passions—good, bad, and ugly—certainly existed, but were usually directed by noneconomic ends. Markets were "accessories of economic life."[26] Even mercantilism left the social landscape relatively unscathed from market patterns. Yet early political economists argued otherwise. Adam Smith famously wrote that the social division of labor depended on already-existing markets, which grew naturally from "man's propensity to barter, truck, and exchange one thing for another." But we are not "bartering savages" as Smith argued—we are cooperative humans. Of

25. Polanyi 2001.
26. Polanyi 2001, 71.

course, for Polanyi, "In retrospect it can be said that no misreading of the past ever proved more prophetic of the future."[27]

Capitalism sought to marketize the ancient orders: to disembed the world, to uproot place, and destroy a communal mode of existence. Polanyi writes of three communal forces that capital wrecked: (1) *Reciprocity,* a territorially bound principle of give-and-take or obligation. (2) *Redistribution,* the sharing and exchange of goods between people, as with potlatch. (3) *Householding* or autarky, the production for one's own needs. Together, these practices helped reproduce self-sufficient human ecosystems. Yet by the nineteenth century, a market logic had exploded, in which gain was the new virtue and greed was the new god. The three dominant social patterns, all of which grounded economic relations, were undermined by market logics that disembedded human activity from the commons. "Instead of economy being embedded in social relations, social relations are embedded in the economic system."[28] The great transformation was a direct attack on humanity's self-sufficiency.

Polanyi further argued that labor, land, and money were remade as "fictitious" commodities. Fictitious, because they were never produced for sale. Take land and labor, both of which are capitalist misnomers. "Land," or property, of course refers to the natural environment, which was never produced for capitalism. The forests and rivers of planet Earth existed for billions of years before the first human breath. "To isolate [land] and form a market was perhaps the weirdest of all the undertakings of our ancestors."[29] And "labor" refers to the rich activity of human beings, who lead colorful physical, psychological, and emotional lives. Neither was made by capital, and both resist commodification. Treating labor and land as commodities subordinates their organic substance, the singular reality of their being, to the market economy. Our social reality de-

27. Polanyi 2001, 45.
28. Polanyi 2001, 59.
29. Polanyi 2001, 187.

pends on the treatment of lands, persons, and animals *for sale,* and this is so destructive to the environment and the human condition.

Capitalism presents itself as a natural social order. But it is a mystical dreamworld. What could be weirder than sticking a barcode on the soils and peoples of the planet? What could be more bizarre than assuming a "self-regulating" market as our god? The fundamental tensions within capitalism arise from its artificial foundations of land (nature) and labor (human being). And Polanyi's analysis provides an inspiration for surviving in and beyond the coming storm: by signaling *a return to embedded economies.* Prior to capitalism, human economies—and their intertwined psychological ecologies—were often centered around reciprocal and autonomous practices. Reversing the toxicity of the market economy has never been more urgent: to create alternative worlds animated by the ancient spirit of reciprocity, redistribution, and autonomy. We must rediscover our territorial dignity.

The Virtual Pauper

"Under capitalism, the only thing worse than being exploited is not being exploited," writes Michael Denning.[30] Work, or starve. This is the brutal contract that capital imposes on our lands, bodies, and minds. The very idea and practice of waged labor completely occupies the horizon of our personal, political, and social imagination. Capitalism has successfully normalized the idea that waged work is natural, and unemployment is unnatural. This dyad of employment and unemployment, and the centrality of the wage, masks important alternatives to capitalism, and the centrality of geographic justice. The fear of "unemployment" is a crushing ideological barrier to change and mystifies the brutal genealogy of capitalism. Yet unemployment is a discursive invention mobilized in the economic slump of 1880s and '90s, and the Great Depression

30. Denning 2010, 79.

of the 1930s. The term enabled the great social-democratic techniques "to contain the spectre of wageless life."[31]

Wageless life, rather than wage labor, is Denning's starting point for understanding capitalism—and one we find invaluable. "Since the beginnings of the wage-labour economy, wageless life has been a calamity for those dispossessed of land, tools, and means of subsistence."[32] Accordingly, Denning argues that an analysis of capitalism must not begin from the accumulation of capital but from its obverse: the accumulation of (landless) labor. We must de-fetishize the wage. "For capitalism begins not with the offer of work, but with the imperative to earn a living. Dispossession and expropriation, followed by the enforcement of money taxes and rent: such is the idyll of 'free labour.'"[33] Pauperism, for example, has always shadowed wealth. And it is the destination of all unemployed laborers. As Marx and Engels write, "The modern laborer . . . sinks deeper and deeper below the conditions of his own class. He becomes a pauper, and pauperism develops more rapidly than population and wealth."[34]

The term "pauper" emerged as far back as the 1510s in legal parlance, referring to a person destitute of property, livelihood, or means of support. The figure of the pauper in the history of English capitalism, writes Polanyi, was regarded as "a social disease which was caused by a variety of reasons, most of which became active only through the failure of the Poor Law to apply the right remedy."[35] Yet the dramatic rise of pauperism is inseparable from capitalist enclosure. "Only in the mode of production based in capital does pauperism appear as the result of labour itself, of the development of the productive force of labour."[36] As Marx

31. Denning 2010, 84.
32. Denning 2010, 79.
33. Denning 2010, 80.
34. Marx and Engels 2015, 19–20.
35. Polanyi 2001, 91.
36. Marx 1973, 604.

further argues, pauperism is a necessary category of the surplus population. "Pauperism is the hospital of the active labour-army and the dead weight of the industrial reserve army. Its production is included in that of the relative surplus population, its necessity is implied by their necessity; along with the surplus population, pauperism forms a condition of capitalist production, and the capitalist development of wealth."[37] To become surplus, one must *always-already be surplus.*

In Marx's earlier writing, captured in the *Grundrisse,* he further argues that the worker and the pauper are *not* so distinct. In fact, the former *includes* the latter.

> It is already contained in the concept of the free labourer, that he is a pauper: virtual pauper. According to his economic conditions he is merely a living labour capacity, hence equipped with the necessaries of life. . . . He can live as a worker only in so far as he exchanges his labour capacity for that part of capital which forms the labour fund. This exchange is tied to conditions which are accidental for him, and indifferent to his organic presence. He is thus a virtual pauper. Since it is further the condition of production based on capital that he produces ever more surplus labour, it follows that ever more necessary labour is set free. Thus the chances of his pauperism increase.[38]

This passage on pauperization is remarkable. Under capitalism, most of us are *virtual paupers*: who we are, our history, our self-worth, is irrelevant to the machinery of extraction and circulation. What matters is our labor power, which we scramble to sell under conditions of duress and unfreedom—although this sale requires a willing buyer! We are thrown into a machinery of dispossession and inequality before our first breath. Before we are laborers we are paupers: we are bare life. In fact, we are laborers *because* we are paupers. As Denning argues, "We must insist that 'proletarian' is not a synonym for 'wage labourer' but for dispossession, expropriation, and radical dependence on the market. You don't

37. Marx 1990, 797.
38. Marx 1973, 604.

need a job to be a proletarian: wageless life, not wage labour, is the starting point in understanding the free market."[39] The necessity to become a wage laborer is violently imposed. While Marx discussed the proletariat in relation to European industrialism—it is a figure of dispossession that cries out well beyond this history and geography. The "free" proletarian is a virtual pauper: without land, liberty, or livelihood.

Some are of us are *virtual* paupers, other are *actualized* paupers—but pauperism is our shared condition of oppression. The virtual pauper forces us to remember what we've forgotten we've forgotten: the original sin of primitive accumulation. It is this alienation that binds us together in existential fraternity. Such an understanding of the pauper dislocates the figure of the wage laborer as the paragon of meaningful work and social dignity.

39. Denning 2010, 81.

A Worldless Planet

Alienation

The existential cost of enclosure and pauperization is a pervasive alienation. Alienation describes the traumatic effect of capitalist production on human beings. Most people's jobs under capitalism are characterized by tedium, apathy, and exhaustion. And that, of course, is for those lucky enough to be exploited by waged life. Marx's basic ontology of capitalism was alienation, even though the term cycled out of his later work. Alienation is a disorienting sense of existential exclusion: to be separated from the material conditions that enable humans to flourish. Our human nature, for Marx, was not a fixed *essence* but a form of *relational existence,* or what he termed "species-being." Species-being is the human capacity to consciously and freely transform the world, through our work, to meet our creative needs. To be alienated is to be denied this liberty of meaningful work: we cannot take hold of the world, our place in it, and insist, *I matter*. The alienated are denied an ability to reshape their simple being-in-the-world. The private ownership of land, labor power, and the means of production, all expropriate our basic human material reality. The surfaces and the folds of existence, the most intimate and the most distant, are all stolen. Relationships severed.

Marx argued that it was not the activity of thinking that was essential to *realizing* ourselves in the world *but conscious productive activity* or *labor*. And our inability to realize ourselves in the world is a great crime of modernity. Human beings are *spatial beings*. But billions are barred from impressing their creative existence into the flesh of the world—instead, they must float along its concrete shells, lost, like so many ghosts.

Unlike other political economists, Marx believed work is not a burden but something to be celebrated. It is the *denial* of our ability to *control* how we work that leads to alienation. The proletariat is forced to work for its survival—for a boss—under conditions of unfreedom. The first form of alienation Marx describes is a loss of control over the *labor process*. "The activity of the worker is not his spontaneous activity. It belongs to another, it is a loss of his self."[1] We must sell our labor power to capitalists to survive, thereby transforming human labor into a "fictitious" commodity. In turn, such work—which has profit as its end rather than human fulfillment—becomes deskilled and homogenized. Workers come to see themselves as merely "abstract activity and a stomach."[2] Speaking of the factory, although it could equally apply to a call center, Marx writes:

> Factory work exhausts the nervous system to the uttermost; at the same time, it does away with the many-sided play of the muscles, and confiscates every atom of freedom, both in bodily and intellectual activity. . . . The special skill of each individual insignificant machine-operator, who has now been deprived of all significance, vanishes as an infinitesimal quantity in the face of the science, the gigantic natural forces, and mass of social labour embodied in the system of machinery, which, together with those three forces, constitutes the power of the "master."[3]

Humans are reduced to a "living appendage of the machine"—and machines, in turn, become their competitors (including, of course, robots). Alienation from the *products of our labor* follows directly from this. We produce commodities for somebody else, and they become external to our effort. Workers become surrounded by, and dominated by, embodiments of their own past—or *dead*—labor. For Marx, "this realisation of labour appears as a *loss of reality* for the worker, objectification as *loss of a bondage to the object,* and

1. Marx 1988, 74.
2. Marx 1975, 285.
3. Marx 1990, 548–49.

appropriation as *estrangement,* as *alienation*."[4] Underpinning this process is a wider culture of commodity fetishism: commodities appear as independent entities without social relations. The object is viewed as possessing a life and value of its own—instead of being a relationship between people. Alienated labor, now alienated from its products, is then made to buy it all back. But it can't.

> It is true that labor produces . . . for the rich wonderful things—but for the worker it produces privation. It produces palaces—but for the worker, hovels. It produces beauty—but for the worker, deformity. It replaces labor by machines—but some of the workers it throws back to a barbarous type of labor, and the other workers it turns into machines. It produces intelligence—but for the worker idiocy, cretinism.[5]

Alienation is not limited to the sphere of production. It soon tears through society: humans become alienated from each other, interacting according to the roles assigned by the capitalist system's division of labor. Instead of interacting with our sisters and brothers as humans (or, as "ends"), we interact with them according to their job titles (or as "means"). Finally, after alienation from our *labor process,* the *objects of our labor,* and our *neighbors,* we at last become alienated from *ourselves.* Our body, our sexuality, our maternal life, is taken from us.[6] We wake up as strangers in a strangle land: where people, work, animals, plants, rivers, homes, and even our minds, fade and retreat from touch. By estranging humans from the world, our very species-being is alienated. Species-being, to recall, is our capacity to transform our worldly conditions of existence through work. "In creating an objective world by his practical activity, in working-up inorganic nature, man proves himself a conscious species being."[7] Species-being is today replaced by animal survivalism—and our ability to creatively and freely play with the world around us is foreclosed. Marx writes that capitalist

4. Marx 1988, 71.
5. Marx 1988, 73.
6. Nast 2017.
7. Marx 1988, 76–77.

political economy "knows the worker only as a working animal—as a beast reduced to the strictest bodily needs."[8]

Most of us know, or *feel,* that something is deeply wrong in everyday life. But understanding where that pain originates is a different matter. There is thus a political and ethical imperative to return to alienation as a grounding point for collective struggle. It diagnoses a deep existential melancholia and unites the concrete and psychic structures of oppression. Mental ill health is so often pathologized as an individual failing. Yet how can someone who is alienated from their entire world *not* be ill? Violent conditions have violent ends.[9] Of course, alienation is itself a source of further capitalist accumulation. Distraction technologies and the entertainment industry sell us meaningless thrills to patch over the pain. We adorn our private comfort capsules and turn ever inwards. The net result is that capitalism, in an admirable circularity, becomes the cause and (temporary) solution of its own discontents.

World Alienation

A planet of surplus populations is a planet of endemic worldlessness. Poverty is not simply an economic malady, it is a form of world alienation. In the shanty towns of a worldwide slum, in the American Rust Belt, at migrant detention facilities, in homeless shelters, in prisons, in ghettos, in *les banlieues,* we discover a pervasive loss of world. World capitalism prevents billions of people from obtaining a *place in the world* from which they can speak and act freely. We are continually denied the ability, under capitalism, to create, use, and inhabit common artifacts, buildings, and spaces. Arendt characterized modern life in terms of this "world alienation," and not, as Marx largely did, as a psychological condition

8. Marx 1988, 29.
9. Laurie and Shaw 2018.

(i.e., the estrangement of species-being). Arendt writes: "World alienation, and not self-alienation as Marx thought, has been the hallmark of the modern age."[10] Of course, capitalism features prominently in both Arendt's and Marx's accounts of alienation: primitive accumulation, the "original sin" of capitalism, is a founding moment of alienation, since it threw people off the land and destroyed their existential autonomy. The creation of a laboring poor is fundamental. As Arendt explains:

> The first stage of this alienation was marked by its cruelty, the misery and material wretchedness it meant for steadily increasing numbers of "laboring poor," whom expropriation deprived of the twofold protection of family and property, that is, of a family-owned private share in the world, which until the modern age had housed the individual life process and the laboring activity subject to its necessities.[11]

Enclosure set in motion a profound world alienation, casting the poor from their place in the world. Instead of property belonging to the commons, it was attached to individual persons. As Arendt states, "Thus modern property lost its worldly character and was located in the person himself."[12] For this reason, Arendt argues that alienation is not simply an inward psychological condition but a loss of world: the deprivation of durable material structures and institutions. Alienation presents as a profound loss of our territorial autonomy—a loss of one's *place in the world,* or "a tangible, worldly place of one's own."[13] This analytic is politically important. Understanding global poverty requires us to look beyond individual "failings" and toward world-alienation.[14] A lack of common property forces the poor into abject conditions. Whether slum dwellers in Dharavi, India, or jobless workers in Glasgow, to call such people "poor" or "unemployed" fails to cap-

10. Arendt 2013, 254.
11. Arendt 2013, 256.
12. Arendt 2013, 70.
13. Arendt 2013, 70.
14. Luttrell 2015.

ture the spatial trauma of their alienation. They have been *denied a right to the world*. And the consequences of worldlessness are felt everywhere: in ruined social housing, ocean waste, atmospheric pollution, river toxicity, a planet of slums, and ongoing crises in mental health.

The enclosure of the commons, the disembedding of the economy, and the pervasive alienation that resulted are overlapping aspects of worldlessness. Individual spheres of togetherness, unique stories-so-far,[15] were bulldozed by the violent equivalences of money. The expropriation of the commons created masses of human beings radically exposed to the exigencies of life: virtual paupers. Deprived of the territory that had ensured their place in the world, the members of this new laboring class were as instrumentalized as the land itself. Instead of building dignified human worlds, *impressing ourselves into the flesh of the world,* we were forced to engage in the activity of mindless, automatic survivalism.

> For even now, labouring is too lofty, too ambitious a word for what we are doing, or think we are doing, in the world we have come to live in. The last stage of the labouring society, the society of jobholders, demands of its members a sheer automatic functioning, as though individual life had actually been submerged in the overall life process of the species and the only active decision still required of the individual were to let go, so to speak, to abandon his individuality, the still individually sensed pain and trouble of living, and acquiesce in a dazed, "tranquillized," functional type of behaviour.[16]

World alienation is the loss of a plural world of experience, social infrastructure, and commons by which our sense of self and reality is established. Whether a slum in the global South, or the city of Flint, Michigan, world alienation can mean a lack of clean water, sustainable food, hygienic living conditions, or shelter. But alienation refers to something more insidious: the cumulative effects of dwelling in cruel ecologies in which we are robbed of our digni-

15. Massey 2005.
16. Arendt 2013, 322.

ty and autonomy—where we can no longer work for and *with* the world and materialize our creativity in shared spaces. This is one of the cruelest aspects of capitalist alienation: the weight of existence is individualizing, rather than distributed amongst worldly coexistents. As Johanna Luttrell writes, when "the body takes the place of a world, and we are thrown inward upon ourselves, we are 'too far in' our bodies, there is no outlet for our needs, imaginings, expressions, our uniqueness and our dignity."[17] Worldlessness means living in a grinding loneliness and obscurity—forced to exist without leaving footprints. Forced to stay invisible.

17. Luttrell 2015, 876–77.

The Geographies of Surplus Life

SURPLUS HUMANITY today finds itself expelled, thrown into a global mass that is surveilled, even hunted, but never considered as redeemable life. Such life can be found in multiple landscapes: ghettos, prisons, refugee camps, Foxconn factories, cobalt mines, borderlands, or ruined social housing. Sassen argues, such "spaces of the expelled" need to be conceptualized: from dead land, to dead water, to dead neighborhoods.[1] The geography of world capitalism is a landscape of segregation: split between fortified interiors and abandoned exteriors. As Davis writes, "With a literal 'great wall' of high-tech border enforcement blocking large-scale migration to the rich countries, only the slum remains as a fully franchised solution to the problem of warehousing this century's surplus humanity."[2]

The Prison

The prison is a key site of surplus populations. Incarceration is a *central* feature of capitalist society. As Sassen writes, "today's prisoners in the United States and in the United Kingdom are increasingly today's version of the surplus laboring population common in the brutal beginnings of modern capitalism."[3] The American criminal justice system imprisons 2.3 million. This is in addition to the 3.7 million people on probation, and 840,000 on parole.[4] The wealthiest country on earth has the highest prison population

1. Sassen 2014, 222.
2. Davis 2006, 201.
3. Sassen 2014, 64.
4. Prison Policy Initiative, 2018.

and incarceration rate among the developed world. "The prison system," write Michael McIntyre and Heidi Nast, "has become a means of warehousing a racialized reserve army of predominantly young male labour."[5] Bauman writes, in support of this idea, that prisons are no longer designed to "recycle" surplus populations back into society: "Explicitly, the main and perhaps the sole purpose of prisons is not just any human-waste disposal but a final, definitive disposal. Once rejected, forever rejected."[6]

The U.S. prison system continues to criminalize poverty and dehumanize many of its inmates. For Laura Hudson writes, "The dehumanization that consigns millions of people to spending their lives in cages allows their suffering to be seen as non-criminal: they are seen as more beast than human. These are populations excised from production, sanctioned by the law, and consigned to bare life."[7] An important example is the California prison system. Ruth Gilmore argues that California's prison system, and political economy, is the site of multiple surpluses: surplus finance capital, surplus land, surplus state capacity, and surplus populations (predominantly Black and Latino men). The prison became a prominent warehouse for California's expelled and insecure lives in the wake of California's economic restructuring in the 1970s. The inmate population soared by 500 percent between 1982 and 2000,[8] even as the crime rate peaked and declined from 1980. Surplus populations that don't make it to the "golden gulag" are managed by military recruitment and urban policing—both have become sites for the extraction of surplus value.[9]

Underpinning the U.S. prison-industrial complex is what Loïc Wacquant calls a *penal state*. Since the 1980s, this state formation has pacified and oppressed surplus populations. "At the lowest

5. McIntyre and Nast 2011, 1517.
6. Bauman 2004, 86.
7. Hudson 2011, 1671.
8. Gilmore 2007, 7.
9. Cowen and Siciliano, 2011.

rung of the social ladder," writes Wacquant, "incarceration serves to physically neutralize and warehouse the supernumerary fractions of the working class."[10] Society's castaways are deemed a security risk, because "they are the *living and threatening incarnation of the generalized social insecurity* produced by the erosion of stable and homogenous wage work."[11] The American penal state is not a response to rising crime, but prevents surplus populations from rebelling against their oppressive conditions in the post–civil rights era. Wacquant argues that the prison is a surrogate ghetto for "Black subproletarian": a punitive method of containment that "offers relief not *to* the poor but *from* the poor, by forcibly 'disappearing' the most disruptive of them."[12] The criminalization of poverty polices social insecurity in an age of rampant expulsion.

The Necropolis

Surplus populations are differentially exploited by a racialized capitalism. And this has long been the case since colonial powers divided the globe between a principally white, European "core" and a Black "periphery." McIntyre and Nast discuss this division with their concepts of the biopolis and necropolis.[13] The biopolis, advancing Foucault's biopolitics[14] is a space of governmentality in which life is *protected*. The necropolis, after Mbembe's[15] work on necropolitics, is instead a space in which life is *exploited* and subject to death. "Historically, the necropolis was borne through displacements, enclosures, and containments, both in the context of slavery, the colony and (initially) the nation-state, albeit to vastly differing geographical degrees."[16] Populations in the necropolis were con-

10. Wacquant 2009, xvi.
11. Wacquant 2009, 4.
12. Wacquant 2009, 294–95.
13. McIntyre and Nast 2011.
14. Foucault 2003.
15. Mbembe 2003.
16. McIntyre and Nast 2011, 1470.

quered, exterminated, and purchased: "necropolitical subjects were rendered a free gift of nature to be taken and used at will."[17] While the biopolis and necropolis are geographically distinct, they are linked through relational spaces of accumulation by dispossession. Thus, British imperialism in Africa paved the streets of London. "The biopolis could not have emerged without massive transfers of value over hundreds of years from the necropolis."[18]

The biopolis and the necropolis now crisscross each other. They exist in the same city. Most in the necropolis are rarely targets of direct violence, but are "let die" with little fanfare. "Letting die is not an apocalypse," writes Tania Li. "It is not a media event, like a massacre, an earthquake, or a famine that kills large numbers in a compressed period of time. Nor is it a Malthusian problem of inadequate global food supply. It is a stealthy violence that consigns large numbers of people to lead short and limited lives."[19] For example, even within a single city, some lives are made to let live, others are let die. Consider Chicago. "African-Americans on the south side of Chicago are 'let die' at around 60 years, while the mostly white, middle-class residents on the city's northwest side can expect to live until the age of 77."[20]

Katharyne Mitchell situates the production of surplus life within an analysis of race and neoliberalism. She explores the garrison state's capacity to exile entire populations defined in advance as "risk failures," leading to "the conceptual and physical banishment of whole populations."[21] In the United States, these failures are overwhelmingly coded as Black bodies in urban spaces. These exiled populations are abandoned by the welfare state but are still stigmatized and targeted by regressive forms of (preemptive) policing. For Bauman, "the American black ghetto has turned

17. McIntyre and Nast 2011, 1472.
18. McIntyre and Nast 2011, 1472.
19. Li 2009, 66–67.
20. Li 2009, 66.
21. Mitchell 2009, 240–41.

purely and simply into, a virtually single-purpose, waste dispos-al tip."[22] Or as Cedric Robinson adds, "Where Blacks were once assured of some sort of minimal existence as a source of cheap labor, mass unemployment and conditions of housing and health that are of near-genocidal proportions obtain."[23] Surplus life is intensely gendered, with women subjected to concentrated levels of (sexualized) violence under a patriarchal system. Consider the reduction of women to what Giorgio Agamben terms "bare life," or politically expendable life: as with murdered sex workers in Vancouver, Canada.[24] Or at Ciudad Juárez, on the Mexico–U.S. border, there has been well-documented cases of femicide.[25] Both cases reproduce a gendered necropolitical order and connect to the everyday domestic violences women endure.[26] As crucial as race, gender, and other dimensions of identity are as markers of social, political, and economic justice, Asad Haider argues for the enduring importance of class (and its entanglements with identi-ty) in both our analyses and practices.[27]

The Slum

The explosion of slums reflects the ongoing urbanization of poverty. Unlike the industrial revolution, urbanization today is radically uncoupled from industrialization. *Cities with no jobs.* For Denning, "Bare life, wasted life, disposable life, precarious life, superfluous life: these are among the terms used to describe the inhabitants of a planet of slums."[28] Slums have become a dumping ground, serving as a warehouse for what Davis calls a "true global residuum lacking the strategic economic power of socialized labor, but massively con-

22. Bauman 2004, 82.
23. Robinson 1983, 318.
24. Pratt 2005.
25. Wright 2011.
26. Pain 2015.
27. Haidar 2018.
28. Denning 2010, 79,

centrated in a shanty-town world encircling the fortified enclaves of the urban rich."[29] Much of the global South lives in slum conditions without access to basic infrastructure. For Laura Hudson, slums and ghettos are "spaces of sequestration where the unproductive proletariat—rejected even as a slave—lives in absolute poverty, a byproduct of capitalism's progress."[30] The urban poor are trapped in an informal and "illegal" world without public services or much chance of escape. The U.S. Pentagon also sees slums as potential breeding grounds for future terrorism and disruption—sites designated as extremely challenging to traditional warfighting tactics.[31]

The slums are contaminated by toxic ecologies—often built upon industrial landscapes, chemical refineries, and other abandoned wilds. *Wasted lands, wasted persons.* Vinay Gidwani and Rajyashree Reddy discuss how in metropolitan India, spaces viewed as "wasteful" are separated, enclosed, or else abandoned, under what they term a "techno-ecological urbanization." This separates two populations: "one, the ecology set of an urban bourgeoisie actively tied into global circuits of capital, whose lives are considered worthy of caring by the state; the other, the ecology set of an urban underclass living off the commodity detritus of these global circuits, whose lives are of indifference to the state."[32] Surplus populations become, in effect, the untouchables: not engaged by biopower or everyday (ethical) encounters. The "haves" of the New Economy have their ecology sets and zones of existence, and the "have-nots" theirs. Flows and encounters between these two bodies are confined, whenever possible, to well defined contact zones. Any spillage beyond sanctioned sites of encounter becomes a source of anxiety for the 'haves.'"[33]

Slums are frequently sites of necropolitical violence. For example, targeted assassinations and disappearances comprise a set of

29. Davis 2004, 179.
30. Hudson 2011, 1677.
31. See https://www.youtube.com/watch?v=gEPdOZbyzbw&t=17s.
32. Gidwani and Reddy 2011, 1640.
33. Gidwani and Reddy 2011, 1646.

policing practices in São Paulo's favelas. Jamie Alves argues that police officers keep communities in a permanent state of terror. He refers to this as the "black necropolis," to signal the spaces of police violence (and police-linked death squads) against Black populations. That is, "black bodies are exploited in low-paid jobs, segregated in favelas, incarcerated, beaten, killed, dismembered, disposed in trash cans, burned and discarded to later resurface as bones in what I name macabre spatialities."[34] This is part of a city-wide necropolitical production of space. But, in turn, the city and its squares can become sites of political struggle against white supremacy by Black women and their families.

34. Alves 2014, 324.

The Wretched of the Earth

Racial Capitalism

There is not, and never was, a straightforwardly "universal" proletariat *identity*. Consider the working class in Victorian England: composed of multiple racial, ethnic, and regional differences. The Irish working classes were even viewed as a different race to their English counterparts. Then, and now, this presents an obstacle to (international) solidarity and fuels what Robinson termed racial capitalism. In his analysis, the proletariat is a *deficient* epistemological category that masks racial inequalities.[1] Robinson argues that by starting with the industrial proletariat so much racial history is bypassed. "Western Marxism," he writes, "has proven insufficiently radical to expose and root out the racialist order that contaminates its analytic and philosophic applications or to come to effective terms with the implications of its own class origins. As a result, it has been mistaken for something it is not: a total theory of liberation."[2]

The longer geohistories of surplus populations begin not with industrial capitalism in England—but rather with the expulsionary geographies of European imperialism and the violent points of contact between Europeans and Blacks.[3] Western historical materialism, for Robinson, erases the experiences of colonial territories, marginalized people, or what Frantz Fanon called the *wretched of the earth*. The racist base of capitalism was formed in *premodern* Europe, installed in the feudal order, and carried through the structures of bourgeois European society.[4]

1. See De Angelis 2010 on the fissures within the "middle class."
2. Robinson 1983, 317.
3. Robinson 1983, 310.
4. Robinson 1983, 28.

Contemporary capitalism, in short, evolved from a world system that depended on circuits of slavery, transatlantic violence, and imperialism. At the very same moment European labor was being thrown off the land and herded into a new industrial order, African labor was forced onto plantations in the U.S. south and throughout the Caribbean, thousands of miles away from home. *Both* were internal to world capitalism, and slavery—like accumulation by dispossession—remains a constant violence.

Consequently, the revolutionary subject of history is not a singularly white European proletariat. Indeed, the industrial revolution was never simply located "in" England: it was stretched across imperial networks of production and exchange. The whole globe, and its people, became sites of capital accumulation. As Robinson argues,

> For 400 years, from the fifteenth to the nineteenth century, while the capitalist mode of production in Europe engulfed agrarian and artisanal workers, transforming them over the generations into expropriated, dependent fodder for concentration in factories, disciplined to the rhythms and turbulences of the manufacturing process, the organizers of the capitalist world system appropriated Black labor power as *constant* capital.[5]

Robinson's vital corrective demonstrates the importance of capital beyond the global North. The rise of capitalism was never just a story about English manufacturing. It was equally a tale of cotton fields in Alabama, slave ships in the Atlantic, and razed villages in Africa.

The Global South

Billions of people are not, and never will be, proletarianized. Marx's claim that "accumulation of capital is therefore multiplication of the proletariat" is precisely what is *not* happening from a global perspective.[6] The global North's trajectory of capitalism

5. Robinson 1983, 309.
6. Marx 1990, 764.

in the twentieth century—from a postwar Keynesianism to a post-1970s neoliberalism—is not a historically or spatially *universal* trajectory. Even throughout capitalism's *longue durée,* wageless life has been the default for most of the global South. As Michael Watts writes, "the normal sense of employment always obscured the armies of the poor who lived outside of the normal world of employment and unemployment."[7] Here, populations are *subjected* to capitalism, but not *subjects* (or *agents*) of capitalism. For Munck, "Decent work . . . has never been the norm in the post-colonial world. Rather, super-exploitation, accumulation through dispossession and what might be called 'permanent primitive accumulation' have by and large prevailed."[8] Most of the planet's populations have been abandoned, exploited, or enslaved by capital without ever being absorbed as wage laborers. Capitalism, of course, benefits from this partial proletarianization: it does not need to pay the full costs for the social reproduction of labor.

The internationalization of capital in the 1980s saw the rise of the "world factory": the relocation of deskilled tasks in manufacturing to lower-wage regions of the world. This outsourcing was oriented by access to cheap labor, and to avoid the legal protections of workers in the global North. Hence, the "winners" of global neoliberalism are countries with the most disciplined labor forces. There is not a single "southern" model for understanding precarity, informalization, or poverty. But Structural Adjustment Programs (SAPs) have been a vital method for installing wretched conditions in the global South. These were conditionalities imposed on loans provided by the International Monetary Fund and the World Bank. The strings attached to these loans included, among numerous other stipulations, the privatization of public services and spaces, and the erosion of workers' rights. "In Latin America," writes Davis, "SAPs (often implemented by military dictatorships) destabilized rural

7. Watts 2011, 73.
8. Munck 2013, 752.

economies while savaging urban employment and housing."[9] The rise of the "informal economy" is partly an *outcome* of the violent conditions of the "formal economy." The declining rights of workers, the vast enclosure of the commons, the shift from subsistence agriculture to cash-crop production, has precipitated an informal, and sometimes desperate, survivalism.

Foreign direct investment in Africa, a continent plundered by European colonialism, has been concentrated in extraction and primary commodity production, often in export-processing zones with lax regulations. But this commodity-driven economic growth has been largely jobless: paid employment remains below 20 percent in most African countries.[10] Capitalist forms of "investment," then, do not simply secure the conditions for a dignified humanity, but the conditions for profit. Life expectancy in many African states has declined during neoliberalism's noble interventions. By 2010, life expectancy had fallen by seventeen years on average in Kenya, South Africa, Mozambique, Zambia, Rwanda, Malawi, Zimbabwe, and Namibia. In seven southern African countries, life expectancy had dropped below forty years.[11] By 2018, average life expectancy in Africa trailed the global average by nine years for males (sixty-one years versus seventy years) and ten years for females (sixty-four years versus seventy-four years).[12]

Slavery

Many economists view slavery as *fundamentally inconsistent* with capitalist development. Other times, slavery is viewed as a moral transgression, a disturbing aberration, executed by those who exploit slaves. Both perspectives render slavery as *exceptional* and separate from the "free" market. Yet recent cases of forced and unfree

9. Davis 2004, 20.
10. Lebaron and Ayers 2013, 881.
11. Lebaron and Ayers 2013, 882.
12. Statista 2018.

labor are bound to neoliberal shifts in relations of production and social reproduction. Indeed, historically, slavery has *always* shadowed capitalism. As Marx himself wrote, "In fact, the veiled slavery of the wage workers in Europe needed the unqualified slavery of the new world as its pedestal."[13] It is vital to establish that capitalism was founded on racism, dispossession, and exploitation. The birth of American capitalism was founded on the obscene profits extracted by chattel slavery. As Edward Baptist writes, "Stories about industrialization emphasize white immigrants and clever inventors, but they leave out cotton fields and slave labor."[14]

The *majority* of capital circuits do not pass between unionized labor and masses of proletarians, but gradations of unfree labor. The capitalist world system has produced dreadful slave conditions across the planet. Slavery is defined by academics as unpaid forced labor. The Global Slavery Index estimates 40.3 million people exist in some form of slavery (of which, 71 percent are women).[15] There is a well-documented literature on the rise of "new," "second," or "modern-day" slavery across Africa, particularly in Mauritania, Niger, Mali, and Sudan. Slavery in Africa is linked to the continent's deepening integration within global capital. Forced labor, writes Manzo, is "a consequence of capitalist development itself and not exogenous to it."[16] Accordingly, "generalisations regarding 'surplus' populations may overlook the ways in which 'surplus' workers are not, in fact, epiphenomenal to capital accumulation. Rather, these workers' unfreedom has been fostered by firms."[17]

Capitalism continues to impose an immense planetary race to the bottom, and slavery is its most severe expression. As power is concentrated in fewer hands, it leads to increased levels of unfreedom everywhere. Rather than being a pervasive aberration, slav-

13. Marx 1990: 925.
14. Baptist 2014, xix.
15. Global Slavery Index 2018.
16. Manzo 2005, 528.
17. Lebaron and Ayers 2013, 883.

ery is very much a *direct response* to global capital. As Marx wrote, "Accumulation of wealth at one pole is therefore, at the same time, accumulation of misery, agony of toil, slavery, ignorance, and mental degradation at the other."[18] The accumulation of wealth in the global North continues to accumulate misery, agony, and slavery in the South. A "free market" should not, therefore, imply a free people. Capitalism exists on a continuum of unfreedom: the divide between slavery and wage slavery is never absolute. For most wage workers—virtual paupers—stripped of any means of subsistence and autonomy, *laboring is compulsory*. The only real difference is that actual slavery is permanent, wage slavery (at least theoretically) is temporary.

The *Lumpenproletariat*

The *lumpenproletariat*—roughly translated as "slum workers," or "ragged workers"—was a term used by both Marx and Engels to describe people existing at the bottom of the surplus population. Marx described the *lumpenproletariat* variously as an *underclass* of thieves and "criminals of all kinds," "living on the crumbs of society."[19] Or consider Engels, who wrote, "The *lumpenproletariat,* this scum of the decaying elements of all classes, which establishes headquarters in all the big cities, is the worst of all popular allies. It is an absolutely venal, an absolutely brazen crew."[20] Even in *The Communist Manifesto,* Marx and Engels were reluctant to assign this "social scum," this "passively rotting mass" with the revolutionary potential as the industrial worker.[21] Yet this too quickly discounts the *lumpenproletariat* as a "dangerous class." The *lumpenproletariat* was treated far more as a *moral category* than it was a (valuable) analytical category.

18. Marx 1990, 799.
19. Marx 2009.
20. Engels 2016.
21. Marx and Engels 2015, 18.

The lines between the pauper, the proletariat, and the *lumpenproletariat,* bleed into each other. For example, as we've already argued—following Marx and Denning—the proletarian is always a *virtual pauper.* The proletariat, in a similar vein, can so easily become the *lumpenproletariat.* The ragged worker who is forced to make ends meet by any means necessary is a common destiny for those who live from paycheck to paycheck. The *lumpenproletariat* is an expansive category with a multitude of persons, stories, communities, and trajectories: anybody is welcome! That does not mean it is inherently revolutionary either, just that it is a multitude that is unpredictable because of its difference. As Marx notes, the *lumpenproletariat* is "thoroughly malleable, as capable of the most heroic deeds and the most exalted sacrifices as of the basest banditry and the foulest corruption."[22] Capitalism produces a range of subject *identities,* including a range of mass-produced personalities and axes of division, but most of us exist from a single subject *position,* and one that shadows us always: the *lumpen*! the pauper!

Frantz Fanon mobilized, or *reclaimed,* the *lumpenproletariat* in his discussion of the psychological and physical effects of the colonized nations in Africa.[23] The *lumpenproletariat* referred to the poorest colonial subjects, and especially the peasantry. He argued that this subject position possessed great revolutionary potential. If an entire people are condemned to an underclass by colonial exclusion, Fanon writes, then even colonized "criminals" possess a conscious—even revolutionary—understanding of their oppression. "For the lumpenproletariat, that horde of starving men, uprooted from their tribe and from their clan, constitutes one of the most spontaneous and the most radically revolutionary forces of a colonized people."[24] The *lumpenproletariat* is a stubborn mass of humanity that evades government control, "like a horde of rats; you may kick them and throw stones at them, but despite your ef-

22. Marx 2009.
23. Fanon 1963.
24. Fanon 1963, 128.

forts they'll go on gnawing at the roots of the tree."[25] If the *lumpen* is effectively mobilized, writes Fanon, "all the hopeless dregs of humanity, all who turn in circles between suicide and madness, will recover their balance, once more go forward, and march proudly in the great procession of the awakened nation."[26]

The Black Panther Party would later adapt the use of the term. In both cases, the revolutionary potential of the *lumpenproletariat* is like the (virtual) pauper: it designates a fundamental and shared injustice of racial capitalism. But that shared injustice is so often kept apart in the minds of the oppressed and by the hands of the oppressors. And so, we must continue to learn from the disparate geographies of the *lumpen* in the global South.

25. Fanon 1963, 129.
26. Fanon 1963: 129.

Sites of Radical Praxis and Survival

IN THIS SECTION, we begin to examine the social strategies of populations that live "outside" and in the "cracks" of capitalism. As should be clear by now, many thrive, and billions survive, in the wastelands of capital, particularly in the global South, although increasingly in every corner of the planet. *Perhaps,* we suggest, it is possible to rebuild the geographies of surplus life into new spaces of hope and dignity. Andre Gorz[1] argues that it is now long past time to move beyond our current conception of "work" (the exchange of labor power for wages) and toward what he characterizes as a culture-based society and multi-activity for everyone. In such a society, what we now think of as work would occupy a much less important role in everyday life. People would then be free to pursue other interests, either individually or in concert with others. Gorz lays out three conditions[2] for exiting the present work-based society and attaining a culture-based (multi-activity) society: (1) Free people's minds and imaginations to explore other forms of cooperation, exchange, and solidarity. (2) Adopt the point of view of a radically different social and economic organization beyond capitalism. (3) Widen the "gap" between society and capitalism to enable alternative socialities to flourish.

For enormous swathes of the population who have long been surplus to capital these conditions, by necessity, are *already* in existence. And for those for whom life as surplus is now coming, these are the new conditions that must be faced. The repertoires and improvisations that make everyday life possible for those outside

---

1. Gorz 1999.
2. Gorz 1999, 78–79.

of waged work might provide key insights for new forms of production, reproduction, and social relations to replace the present
(but rapidly disappearing) arrangements—even if these alternate
forms are now often produced in brutal and exigent circumstances. As Sassen writes, "the spaces of the expelled cry out for conceptual recognition. They are many, they are growing, and they are
diversifying. They are conceptually subterranean conditions that
need to be brought above ground."[3] Sassen argues that these are
potentially "new spaces for making" local economies and communities. But just how is left untheorized. Accordingly, rather than
viewing the present conjuncture as requiring increased inclusion
in the labor-based society and its necessary forms of exploitation,
we examine how it might be possible to recast salutary forms of
(re)production that until now have been largely coerced imposi-
tions into positively inflected, freely chosen opportunities. Our
point, here, is to listen and learn from those who have never been
proletarianized to reimagine what may be possible.

Strategies of the Surplus

In this section we do not catalogue in great detail the day-to-day
provisioning activities of so-called surplus populations, since a
great deal of empirical scholarship already exists. Consider the
following inventory from Jan Breman, who describes the irregular
employment of casual day laborers, cleaners, garbage collectors,
street vendors, or construction workers:

> The working men, women, and children are sometimes needed in
> the towns and sometimes in the countryside. Sometimes they are put
> to work in the obscure and degraded landscape in between these two
> extremes . . . They live and work at these sites for as long as the job
> lasts. The rest of the time they are confined in slum-like sprawling
> settlements on the fringes of villages, squatting with no legal title,
> waiting until the call comes for them to leave again. . . . Yet the fact

3. Sassen 2014, 222.

that these people are hidden away from mainstream society in colonies and transit camps is no reason to label them as marginal or
peripheral. They are a vast army of reserve labour at the heart of the
predatory capitalism that emerged so virulently on the subcontinent
of South Asia in the second half of the twentieth century.[4]

This kind of characterization of the quotidian conditions for much
of the world's population, though poignant and compelling, provides
only a partial representation of how people actually "get by" in the
world. It is the widely varying set of social relations within which
these activities are embedded, for better or worse, that begins to
flesh out how these individual and collective biographies are produced. It is also out of these myriad arrangements that insights
might be elicited to inform the life chances for the new masses
being made surplus by late capitalism. In the space available, we
offer what we hope are a number of provocative samples. These run
on a spectrum from the brutal repression of surplus populations at
one end (including, of course, the uncounted numbers of annual
fatalities attributable to the mundane workings of the present system), to full and formal integration at the other end. In elaborating
these more enabling potentialities, we align our assessment with
AbdouMaliq Simone's proposition (gleaned through several decades
of work in urban areas of Southeast Asia and Africa):[5]

This is in no way to celebrate the resilience or tactical brilliance of
the urban poor—the clever way they manage to eke out an existence
in conditions of chronic scarcity and exploitation. There is no ro-
mance here. Rather, I consider the intricate interweaving of the poor
into the material and social milieu where it is not easy to quickly
decide unequivocal relations of power, advantage, or deprivation.[6]

Much of Simone's work on the complex geographies of the urban
poor, while cognizant of these dire conditions, has demonstrated a
rich and nuanced tapestry of relations between the poor and other

4. Bremen 2016, 257.
5. Simone 2001; 2013; 2015; 2016.
6. Simone 2015, S 15.

populations within cities and their expanding peripheries. Many of these observations emerge from Simone's focus on the necessary densities and propinquities created in contemporary urban settings:

> While homogenous basins of impoverishment certainly exist as spatially marginal from the various real economies of urban life, the probable majority of the poor in Jakarta [among many other examples] are inserted in highly variegated, heterogeneous interactions with others whose income levels and access to assets and resources cover a wide range of possibilities. . . . This juxtaposition is no guarantee that the eventual prospects of any specific poor household would be inevitably enhanced or their security strengthened. But it does point to the necessity of considering the existence of the urban poor within a broader range of economic and social interrelationships, making general statements about the characteristics, expendability, or precarity of the urban poor of limited value.[7]

In a similar vein, writing about Nouakchott in Mauritania, Choplin and Ciavolella note that "urban margins become laboratories for new shared identities and social solidarities and thus, perhaps, for the formation of a new political subject."[8] It is this set of necessary interactions, and the manifold interdependencies represented by them, that give Simone and many other scholars cause for some optimism that more inclusive social relations are possible.

In what follows, we offer five specific examples of the survival strategies of surplus populations. Our goal is not to supply a comprehensive inventory but to illustrate instances in which typical binaries are breached, and which may offer bases for new solidarities across long-standing divides: such as formal/informal economies, production/social reproduction, race/class, and so on. The first four cases are not instances of moving beyond or outside of capitalism but are rather bricolages (making do) within the system.[9] They are not clear attempts at autonomous control of the means and ends of

---

7. Simone 2015, S 16–17.
8. Choplin and Ciavolella 2017, 329.
9. De Certeau 1984.

(re)production, but include insights into strategies of cooperation and expropriations of the expropriators. These four examples focus on urban settings. Though there are many instances of rural and agrarian movements thriving beyond capitalism (e.g., the Landless Workers Movement in Brazil, the Naxalite movement in India, and so on), it is clear that ongoing waves of dispossession are forcing more of the world's surplus humanity into urban settings unable to absorb them in historical sectors of waged labor.[10] In the nascent efforts highlighted in the first four cases we can see glimmers of strategies that will become increasingly necessary as more of us become surplus. Finally, our fifth case focuses on the Zapatista liberation in Chiapas, Mexico, to illustrate a much more fully developed vision of a world beyond capitalism, which engages with the vital issues of territorial autonomy.

A common strategy of surplus populations is differing attempts at reclaiming (often meager) common wealth in the face of historical and ongoing dispossessions at various scales, from the global to the body.[11] Each of our cases demonstrates a form of *communing*—usually claiming some form of public space—in the face of repeated privatizations and deprivations. These short vignettes resonate with recent work by Hardt and Negri in terms of entrepreneurship from the bottom.[12] But as Massimo De Angelis puts it, effective efforts at commoning will have to go much further:

> To turn a noun into a verb is not a little step and requires some daring. Especially if in doing so we do not want to obscure the importance of the noun, but simply ground it on what is, after all, life flow: there are no commons without incessant activities of commoning, of

10. In urban areas, in both the global North and South, there are also numerous examples of people reclaiming autonomy and control over resources and skills. These take many forms ranging from community gardens to local banking to worker-controlled enterprises, and many more. One very useful entrée into these experiments is The Next System Project, accessible at https://thenextsystem.org/.

11. Sevilla-Buitrago 2015.

12. Hardt and Negri 2017.

(re)producing in common. . . . The positing for today of the question
of what form of commoning, of (re)producing in common, and the
field of common rights as distinct from legal rights, means therefore
that we cannot separate the question of autonomy, community, life
flow, and ecology, but must assert them all at once while struggling
for livelihoods.[13]

And further:

the process of commoning beyond capital is a process of destructive
creation as opposed to the process of creative destruction of Schum-
peterian memory. While for the latter the creation of the new and
the correspondent destruction of the old is concerned with the mu-
tation of the forms of capitalist social relations, we can understand
the concern of destructive creation, the destruction of these very
capitalist relations and the correspondent creation of new forms of
commoning predicated on different value productions.[14]

As we think about the new forms of provisioning and livelihood
that the future of surplus humanity will necessitate, we must remain cognizant of the theoretical, conceptual, and practical dif-
ficulties that actual, on-the-ground commoning will entail. As
McCarthy reminds us: "What unites most of these calls for new
commons is not so much a coherent vision of common property regimes, as their assertion of collective ownership and rights
against relentless privatization and commodification."[15] Drawing
on the extensive common pool and common property literature,
he also helpfully enumerates several facets of commoning that
will require our committed attention:

One is the need to define and justify the criteria for membership of a
commons (because the other face of membership is exclusion). Another is the need to define the spatial scale of the commons, and to
grapple with whether the operative social and biophysical scales are
remotely in alignment. A third is the need to examine what other
claims the new "commons" excludes or overrides. A fourth is to spell

13. De Angelis 2010, 955–956.
14. De Angelis 2010, 959.
15. McCarthy 2005, 11.

out how the commons will intersect with whatever states also claim authority over the resource or territory in question. Perhaps most important is the need to spell out why a common property regime is expected to lead to better social and environmental outcomes than state or private ownership.[16]

An important point to note here is that the act of commoning for some requires a simultaneous act of enclosure to others. The ethics of commoning is located precisely in this act of opening-and-closing. This disturbs the typical binary of enclosure/dispossession versus commoning/reappropriation so prevalent in the scholarly literature. It also complicates the question of *who* favors or opposes enclosure and/or commoning. As Hall tells us:

> The return to primitive accumulation has reminded us of what is hidden by liberal narratives of markets as uncoerced, voluntary spheres of interaction. History continues very often to be written in Marx's letters of blood and fire. This, however, is not the whole of the story. When the fact that markets often have their origins in coercion becomes an assumption that people will only engage in markets when forced to do so, things have gone too far. If an oppositional politics of primitive accumulation assumes that people are entirely opposed to markets, commodities, and private property, and wish to live their lives entirely within the commons, that politics will not find a great deal of support.[17]

Urban Survival: Four Cases

Cusco, Peru, is the site of our first example. In a recent article on street vending, Griet Steel uses Cindi Katz's tripartite classification of resilience, reworking, and resistance to examine the activities of individual, itinerant sellers. As Steel notes:

> In her examples of resilience, she refers to small instances of recuperation and re-articulation, which enable people to get by each day. "Reworking" refers to situations in which people successfully alter their conditions of existence. Katz . . . talks in terms of resistance

16. McCarthy 2005, 24.
17. Hall 2012, 1205.

only in cases where "reworking reorders and undermines the structural constraints that affect everyday life to make it more livable and to create viable terrains of practice" or where "historical and geographical conditions of oppression and exploitation are undermined at various scales."[18]

Particularly for itinerant street vendors (as opposed to those with fixed locations from which organized resistance is more easily coordinated), Steel argues that individual acts of resilience and (some) reworking are the predominant strategies. For example, while vendors who had affiliated with associations were eventually allowed—by municipal authorities in acknowledgment of their vital role in the tourist economy—to purchase permanent stalls in central market locations, itinerant vendors were excluded from similar public schemes for greater security. Because they lack the organizational power, itinerant street vendors tend to resort to practices of resilience and reworking: they defend each other against theft; provide access to informal savings and credit systems; loan each other small sums of money; and "expand their 'social security' network in general."[19] While these conditions and social relations are far from ideal, these forms of cooperation and interdependence do allow these "surplus" people to exist in the tourist centers vital to their ability to "get by" even in the face of sustained and repressive state strategies of exclusion.

Our second case—which moves us a bit further along the spectrum toward legitimate integration with the formal economy—is a recent study of informal service sector providers and the "new middle class" in Delhi, India. In language that resonates with the possibilities articulated in much of Simone's work, Schindler[20] draws not so much on the victimization of the urban poor (without diminishing the importance of these repressive processes) but rather on the evolving symbiotic relations between the urban poor and the emerging middle class.

18. Steel 2012, 1010; quoting Katz 2004, 251.
19. Steel 2012, 1016.
20. Schindler 2014, 570–71.

Schindler describes

> the changing nature of urban poverty in India, as the poor in many
> cities are increasingly turning to the informal service sector (ISS) for
> their livelihoods. . . . Alternatively, demand for services from the new
> middle class has "pulled" the poor into the ISS. . . . the new middle
> class and urban poor are drawn together in ways that render them
> interdependent—their interaction allows the new middle class to
> practice particular lifestyles, while the urban poor are able to secure
> livelihoods.[21]

And finally,

> The new middle class requires the production of world-class spac-
> es where its members can display the particular behavioral charac-
> teristics that affirm their class membership. By employing domestic
> servants and other informal service providers members of the new
> middle class affirm their class membership.[22]

To make this relationship workable, the middle class tries to regulate the use of public space by the poor. They keep them close
enough to provide services, but under regulations and conditions
that maintain a middle-class sense of "order." In the trade-off, the
middle class display their status, and the poor are able to subsist.
Clearly these kinds of interclass relations are extremely widespread (and increasing) and can be instrumental in blurring the
lines between the formal and informal economies, between production and (social) reproduction, as well as forcing the recognition of the mutual dependency and co-constitutive natures of
what are typically viewed as bitterly contending factions. While
not ideal in any sense, these relations (which exist virtually everywhere)[23] are significantly more anodyne than the brutal repression with which one end of our spectrum is anchored.

A third case study is documented in Lindell's assessment of new
spaces, tactics, and scales of organizing among informal workers

21. Schindler 2014, 558.
22. Schindler 2014, 570.
23. See Buckley 2013; Pratt, Johnson, and Banta 2017; but also see De
Angelis 2010 on the need to "explode" the middle class.

in Africa.[24] This includes reframing discourses that criminalize informality; asserting that informal work forms integral and essential parts of national economies; breaking down sharp divides between formal and informal work and what counts as work; and establishing much wider and broader connections with other sectors of civil society (social movements, NGOs, etc.). Among the other effects of these efforts at redefinition and reframing are attempts by informal workers to align with trade unions, furthering solidarity and potentially strengthening both sides (though the realities of conflicting interests cannot be elided). Lindell also pays close attention to the inherent heterogeneity of the informal sector, which gives rise to very substantial differences in terms of subjectivity, forms of employment, and politics. In the latter, politics cannot be thought of as only a class politics, since the informal sector is multiclassed as well as multioppressed. For example: "cognisance that disadvantaged women in the informal economy are often subject to both economic exploitation and patriarchal oppression has prompted the creation of organisations such as the Self-Employed Women's Association (SEWA) in India, which describes itself as both a union of the self-employed and a women's movement."[25]

Crucially, Lindell describes efforts by informal workers to scale up their organizational efforts in response to the globalized extent of neoliberal, late capitalism, and usefully identifies multiple examples. Again, without romanticizing these achievements, it is possible to discern strategies, with appropriate modifications, for the restructuring of social relations that will be necessary if more and more people are to be able to survive and thrive beyond waged labor.[26]

The fourth case documents a dramatic evolution in the status of garbage scavengers (*cartoneros*) in Buenos Aires, Argentina as

24. Lindell 2010.
25. Lindell 2010, 211. On this intersectionality between class and gender oppression see also Fernandez 2018.
26. Chen, Bonner, and Carré 2015 provide a global overview of recent informal work sector organizing.

they and their activities moved from being prohibited and illegal
to a formal and legally sanctioned social service. All of this oc-
curred by shifting from views of waste materials, and those who
collect them, as *valueless* to a perspective in which both the materials themselves and those involved in their collection were re-
configured as *valuable*. In this study, Whitson contextualizes the
struggles of *cartoneros* to not only survive but alter their own, precarious (in every sense) position within society:

> Like garbage scavengers elsewhere, cartoneros in Argentina earn a
> living by sorting through household and commercial waste in order
> to find recyclable material. Deriving their name from the most com-
> monly collected material—carton, or cardboard—the cartoneros also
> collect paper, metal, glass, and plastic, all items that are sold to re-
> cycling centers for processing and resale for use in the formal man-
> ufacturing sector . . . Their work is both precarious and dangerous:
> not only is the work of cartoneros entirely informal, but it was also
> illegal in Buenos Aires until very recently. Cartoneros additionally
> suffer from exposure to health hazards, harassment by police, and
> other types of abuse.[27]

The conditions that led to the current arrangements follow a quite
typical neoliberal trajectory. Prior to 1976, informal scavenging and
waste collection were often legal and encouraged. With the ad-
vent of the military government, Argentina engaged in successive
rounds of modernization and privatization, including transformations in the waste management sector. Garbage collection was
turned over to a semi-state agency, and informal waste scavenging
and collection was criminalized. These circumstances prevailed
until the economic crash of 2002. Then, as Whitson explains, the
cash economy (on which poor, informal workers were particularly reliant) collapsed and unemployment rates rose to over 50
percent nationwide. All of this led to an increase in the number
of *cartoneros* from 10,000 in Buenos Aires in 2001 to over 40,000
by late 2002.[28] As the economic crisis deepened, the privatization

27. Whitson 2011, 1404–5.
28. Whitson 2011, 1408–9.

scheme for waste collection also deteriorated to the point that in 2002 the City of Buenos Aires passed the Cartoneros Law, which allowed informal workers to again collect and recycle waste materials.[29] This law also decriminalized informal trash collection, and a subsequent law passed in 2005 actually gave formal recognition to the vital role played by the *cartoneros* in urban sustainability.

But, of course, this is not the end of the story. In the post-2005 period, the state has endeavored to keep waste and the *cartoneros* as invisible as possible, through regulating the time and place of their activities (confined principally to authorized recycling centers) to minimize contact between the *cartoneros* and the rest of the population. To a significant extent, however, the circumstances of this case point to the possibility, yet again, of renegotiating the boundaries between the informal and formal economies, between production and reproduction, and between worthy, waged labor and worthless, wageless life. Such blurring and reconfiguring are essential to the task of creating the new imaginaries that will be necessary in a world of reclaimed work. In themselves, of course, the characteristics embodied in these cases are insufficient for the transformations that will be required for existing and emerging surplus humanity to survive and thrive.

The Zapatistas

Our fifth and final case incorporates critical dimensions lacking in the foregoing examples. The most important are issues of territory and autonomy. These are integral elements for reimagining lives and livelihoods, but are often bound together in complicated and troubled ways, with either states or markets (or usually both) impeding their smooth articulation. As Chatterton proposes: "Autonomy is always a tendency, a partially fulfilled desire that is fought for and struggled over. The concepts of survival, self-

29. Whiston 2011, 1409.

management and the common create the wider frame. . . . What we see among those struggling for autonomy is an impulse to find creative survival routes out of the capitalist present, through a rejection of hierarchy and authoritarianism, and a belief in collective self-management."[30]

What most often obstructs the achievement of autonomy is the inability to control territory (as both symbolic and material manifestation of unalienated means of production). Sevilla-Buitrago puts the matter as follows:

> Before enclosure, practices of commoning shape space on a local, use value–oriented basis, generating a spatiality of difference. By invoking the figure of a "universal territorial equivalent" I denote a logic mobilizing abstraction to make the widest possible scope of those diverse social spaces commensurable so they become more easily governable and exchangeable. "Territorial equivalence" refers here to a strategic operational and regulatory rationality that allows maneuvering across heterogeneous types and manifestations of space, rendering them legible for state administration and market mechanisms . . . enclosure can be understood as a process of spatially orchestrated dispossession, aimed at dismantling autonomous, collectively produced and managed forms of common wealth and value regimes.[31]

Finally, and congruent with Sevilla-Buitrago's allusions here to the necessary juridical dimensions of territory and autonomy, we must contend with the seeming unavoidability of the state. As Parenti starkly argues (and representing the views of many like-minded analysts):

> While the state remains important and will likely grow more important, it has for many left scholars and activists withered as an object of serious study or as a political target and prize. But the state cannot be avoided. For left politics to be effective, movements must create strategies that engage and transform the state. Consider for example the anti-statist politics of John Holloway. Influenced by the Zapatistas and influential upon the Occupy movement, Holloway ar-

30. Chatterton 2010, 899.
31. Sevilla-Buitrago 2015, 1001–2.

gues that a "world worthy of humanity cannot be created through the state." . . . His preferred means, a negation: "We start from the scream . . . Faced with the mutilation of human lives by capitalism, a scream of sadness, a scream of horror, a scream of anger, a scream of refusal: NO." . . . This brings to mind Lenin's mocking title, "Left-Wing Communism: An Infantile Disorder" and his chiding of the German ultra-left for having "mistaken their desire, their politico-ideological attitude, for objective reality." . . . For better or worse, the state remains central to modern political struggle.[32]

Here, rather than engaging with one of the fundamental tenets of the Zapatista effort (i.e., *sidestepping* rather than engaging, challenging, or overthrowing the state), Parenti simply elides the question with an unhelpful "pragmatism." The success or failure of the Zapatista experiment on this question concerning the state remains open. For the moment, and at a minimum, the aspirations and already accomplished achievements of the Zapatistas provide an opening to an alternative vision of making lives and worlds.

Beyond, between, and beside world capitalism exists a range of different cosmologies. One of the most successful *worldings* has been the Zapatista peasant liberation in Chiapas, Mexico. The Zapatistas are one example, and there are many, of indigenous groups reclaiming their *territorial* and thus *existential* autonomy. Marx was largely unsympathetic to the European peasantry, perceiving them as unable to form a cohesive, class-conscious political project. But there is much to be gleaned from a peasant cosmology for political praxis and autonomy beyond capitalism: new associations between humans and nonhumans, as well as innovative forms of value and exchange.[33] As one Zapatista put it: "the left has not completely understood the indigenous movement; they are illiterate in terms of autonomy and that we as indigenous people are fundamental to the fight against capitalism."[34]

32. Parenti 2015, 829–30, quoting Holloway 2002, 1; and Lenin V I 1940 (1920), 41.
33. Araujo 2017.
34. Quoted in Mora 2007, 66.

In the face of violent repression from the Mexican authorities, the Zapatista movement has enrolled hundreds of thousands of people in the building of another, more dignified world.

The Zapatistas, who are composed mainly of rural indigenous people, exist across Mexico's southeastern state of Chiapas. Their rebellion and call for territorial autonomy began in 1994 after NAFTA was signed by the Mexican government—a neoliberal project they rightfully predicted would lead to soaring inequality. Their subsequent thirty-year struggle is part of a five-hundred-year history of anticolonialism, including the peasant wars of Emiliano Zapata in the Mexican Revolution. "Before the Zapatista Army for National Liberation was created, we indigenous peoples of Chiapas didn't exist for the capitalist system. It didn't consider us people, we weren't human. It considered us less than trash."[35] The Zapatistas share an antiglobalization, antineoliberalism stance with libertarian socialism and libertarian Marxism, but their wider Mayan cosmology defies political categorization. In the *Fourth Declaration of the Lacandón Jungle* in 1996, they state: "In the world we want many worlds to fit." We can thus see tantalizing glimpses of what is possible if our political goals are for autonomous control of territory and resources—rather than seizing state power or redistributing capital.

The Zapatistas see capitalism as a global monster, a "Hydra" with many heads that feeds on death and destruction. "Every day, at every hour, in every corner of the planet, the Hydra rises again, rejuvenated and hungry. It then bites, swallows, and vomits only to begin the cycle all over again, but with a new face."[36] Accordingly, the Zapatistas understand capital as fighting an endless war against humanity, described in the 2005 *Sixth Declaration of the Selva Lacandona* as "a war of conquest of the entire world, a world war, a war being waged by capitalism for global domina-

35. Moises 2016, 59.
36. Galeano 2016, 198.

tion." Such a war is designed to install capital in every corner of the planet, dispossessing millions of lives.

> As if it were giant vacuum cleaner, capitalism sucks up massive quantities of labor and extracts as much as possible from it, leaving behind nothing but skin and bones. Then it pushes the "eject" button and spits out millions of unemployed people. It is like in the great wars that absorb goods, soldiers, weapons, and territories, and then spit out rubble and corpses. That is why we say that the capitalist machinery is also, and above all, a warlike machine; it is at war—against those who work.[37]

The Zapatistas are well organized across thirty-eight autonomous municipalities in the Highland and Lacandón jungle regions. Central to their success has been long-term grassroots organizing, a form of coexistence based on commons, autonomy, and Zapatismo as a political imaginary.[38] Implementing another world, of course, takes time. "The System does not fear social explosions, as massive and bright as they may be. If a government were to fall, there's always another one waiting on the shelves as a replacement and as another imposition. What terrifies the system is the perseverance of rebellion and resistance from below."[39] Zapatismo was, from the outset of the *First Declaration for the Lacandón Jungle* in 1993, oriented by "struggles for work, land, housing, food, health care, education, independence, freedom, democracy, justice, and peace." Their initial goal of seizing state power soon switched to a broader goal of controlling territorial resources to enable political autonomy. In short, as the Zapatistas evolved, so did their objectives: (1) An agrarian revolution that seized land from primarily mestizo farmers. (2) An institutional politics of self-governance. (3) Making global connections with anticapitalist campaigns.[40]

At the heart of the Zapatista's anticapitalist project is *existential autonomy* beyond the state. To be autonomous is not the same

37. Galeano 2016, 268.
38. Khasnabish 2017, 123.
39. Galeano 2016, 159.
40. Mora 2015.

as being individualist. It requires community organization for the long term. A *fight for common resources* and *independence*. As one member stated, "For us, autonomy is the heart and soul of our resistance. It is a new way of doing politics. It is part of the construction of democracy, justice, and dignity."[41] The Zapatistas seek to reclaim control of their livelihoods, their knowledges, their commons. The ongoing threat posed by Zapatista autonomy is its ability to refuse state and corporate legitimacy by *unplugging* from capitalist realism—legally, imaginatively, institutionally, and materially. This is realized by building new infrastructural and institutional commons such as schools, clinics, and farms. The commons are the backbone of their worlds. Over the past three decades, the Zapatistas "have built clinics, schools, governance structures, and an economy that is accountable to the communities themselves and run according to the radically democratic, anticapitalist principles of the Zapatista struggle."[42] This method of autonomous government—letting the people decide—stems from centuries of indigenous resistance.

The struggle for existential autonomy is always a question of territory. Land is a central component of their fight. "Zapatismo believes that, 'When the land hurts, everything hurts.'"[43] Indigenous self-determination and neo-peasant ontologies are so vital because they lodge the existential struggle within the flesh of the planet—rather than the rigged system of capitalist realism. The Zapatistas demonstrate that wageless life is not worthless life. To be cash-poor is not the same as being resource-poor.[44] Everything stems from the commons, from the planet's soil, rivers, forests, and skies, which have taken billions of years to fruit. The base of the Zapatista's economic resistance is Mother Earth. Their ongoing survival depends on coexisting with Mother Earth:

41. Quoted in Mora 2007: 64
42. Khasnabish, 2017, 123.
43. Galeano 2015, 254.
44. Araujo 2017.

the Zapatistas exercise their *right to the world,* their right to autonomy. As Subcomandante Moises puts it, "Mother Earth is what
gave us life even though there wasn't any government, any gov-
ernors or mayors taking us into account. We were forgotten."[45]
Adding, "There is one thing that unites us in struggle in the coun-
tryside and in the city: we must free ourselves and Mother Earth
from capitalism. Capitalism is destroying Mother Earth and it is
destroying our lives as the exploited of the world."[46] Zapatismo
plants dignity in the simple act of being-in-the-world.

45. Moises 2016, 60.
46. Moises 2016, 312.

Reclaiming Desire

Cruel Optimism

In this section, we argue that capitalism captures our innermost desires and dreams—rendering alternatives unthinkable. Capitalism has failed most people—and now drags billions to disaster. But it not *inevitable* that a planet of surplus populations poses any threat to the horror of capitalism. This is the dilemma we confront. As Gilles Deleuze and Félix Guattari ask, "after centuries of exploitation, why do people still tolerate being humiliated and enslaved, to such a point, indeed, that they *actually want* humiliation and slavery not only for others but for themselves?"[1] This section is driven by precisely this question: given the vast blocs of wasted lives across the planet—in the magnitude of billions—how does capitalism survive *and* continue to reproduce itself? Why, despite the tremendous violence of capital, do people still *desire* it, acting against their mental and physical health? We thus argue for the centrality of desire to understanding capital. Desire is the productive force, impulse, or affective power that connects bodies together (both human and nonhuman). And while surplus populations may embody an incredible, potential power to destabilize the order of things, this desire will remain dormant—or appropriated by fascists—without liberatory alternatives.

The grip that capitalism holds over our dreams and desires is a powerful source of its own self-legitimation: the ideological dyad of employment–unemployment imprisons our minds in a labyrinth of paychecks and bills. This means that the imagination is a crucial battleground for liberation. "In recent decades," writes

1. Deleuze and Guattari 2004, 31.

Andy Merrifield, "it's been incredible how much the imagination seems to have disappeared from left consciousness . . . It is the left's imagination, rather than the state, that seems to have withered away."[2] We must reclaim the politics of the mind and nourish it with fresh, liberatory resources. Challenging "common sense"[3]—both what counts as the "sensible" and what counts as "sensuous"—has never been more important.

Capitalism is not only an economic mode of production but a *mode of existence*. It targets our psychic realities and innermost desires. Marx wrote that capitalism "converts the worker into a crippled monstrosity . . . through the suppression of a whole world of productive drives and inclinations."[4] Félix Guattari likewise wrote that capitalism targets gigantic aggregates of subjective reality, enmeshing itself in our lived, psychic ecologies. It haunts our waking life. For this reason, writes Guattari, "It has become imperative to confront the effect of capitalist power on the mental ecology of daily life."[5] Indeed, the struggle against capital is a battle against a melancholic world: full of alienated, isolated, anxious, depressed, even suicidal populations. More than 300 million people now live with depression, an increase of more than 18 percent between 2005 and 2015.[6]

How does a system built on such misery persist? First is the fundamental problem of misrecognition. Many people fail to even recognize their deep unhappiness within capitalism. And this is not surprising, given capital's rabid scramble to mask our gloom. Those on the inside of capitalism are forced to dwell in a shopping-mall purgatory of fake, shallow satisfaction. Second, even when our *social* ills are documented, they are misdiagnosed as *individual* ills: mental-health problems are shoved within isolated skulls. *The*

2. Merrifield 2011, 145.
3. Gramsci 1971.
4. Marx 1990, 481
5. Guattari 2008, 138–39.
6. World Health Organization 2017; see also Fisher 2009.

problem is with you and not the violent conditions that engulf you.[7] This denies the political radicality of alienation to shake the socioeconomic order. Third, alternatives to capitalism are rendered unimaginable. The endless refrain of *jobs, jobs, jobs* drown other alternatives. Capitalism, in short, hides its ills, fosters misdiagnoses of its pathologies, and prevents any treatment. And so, we keep on desiring that which is unhealthy for us. This is what Berlant terms cruel optimism: "when something you desire is actually an obstacle to your flourishing."[8]

We thus need to focus the terrain of struggle to the desiring subject. This represents a movement from capital-centric approaches, toward understanding the mental ecologies of surplus populations. We require an exit strategy to mobilize the revolutionary force of desire. By tackling capitalist desire head-on, we can address its seeming indomitable grip on our political imaginations and subjective states. This requires decolonizing our minds of the entrenched common sense of what constitutes meaningful work and its connection to happiness, identity, and self-worth. A creative, joyous, and imaginative unlocking of desire for another world requires us to reclaim the landscapes of common sense. To recall Michel Foucault, "Do not think that one has to be sad in order to be militant, even though the thing one is fighting is abominable."[9]

Capitalist Realism

Do we even *know* we are inside a manufactured reality called capitalism? Like a fish in the sea, most of us fail to see the water in which we swim (and the rising temperature!). Capitalism has conquered so many worlds, has seeped into the pores of our skin, the recesses of our imaginations, and the shadows of our dreams. That it is easier to imagine the end of the world than the end of

---

7. Laurie and Shaw 2018.
8. Berlant 2011, 1.
9. In Deleuze and Guattari 2004, xv.

capitalism defines what Fisher calls capitalist realism. Capitalist realism is "the widespread sense that not only is capitalism the only viable political and economic system, but also that it is now impossible even to imagine a coherent alternative to it."[10] *There is no alternative!* Yet the reality we experience is not the only possible reality—it is a fantasy of the ruling classes, a materialization of a mode of existence that is toxic and unstable. Capitalism's brute survivalism, naked ambition, and toxic *ressentiment* have robbed the political imagination. "Capitalism seamlessly occupies the horizons of the thinkable"[11]—particularly in the global North but also in the manufactured aspirations for many in the global South.

Capitalism is a fabricated worldview. Yet its success, to date, has depended on its elimination of itself as a (consciously understood) ideology. The supposedly postideological and postpolitical reality we find ourselves in today is nothing other than the death of imagination and the ascent of *cynicism* as a mode of being-in-the-world. Both present big challenges for mobilizing a planet of surplus populations. The trouble with cynicism is that regardless of our interior subjective beliefs, we still *obey* and keep the gears of the system grinding. Cynics are miserable in their enlightenment, living, breathing, and supporting a reality they know to be toxic. That one can exist with a cynical distance from capitalism does not, therefore, provide an escape hatch but rather supports its very survival. As Slavoj Žižek argues, cynicism is a form of enlightened false consciousness.[12] Inverting Marx's classic formulation of the commodity fetish *(They do not know it, but they are doing it)*, the cynic *knows* very well what they are doing, but still, they are doing it.

The keystone of capitalist realism remains the utter worship of paid work. As Merrifield observes,

> work is revered in our culture, yet at the same time workers are becoming superfluous; you hate your job and your boss, hate the ser-

10. Fisher 2009, 2.
11. Fischer 2009, 8.
12. Žižek 1989.

vility of what you do, and how you do it, the pettiness of the tasks involved, yet want [need?] to keep your job at all costs. You see no other way of defining yourself other than *through work,* through what you do for a living, through the "honor" of being employed.[13]

If capital has robbed us of our imagination—a form of epistemic dispossession[14]—it is vital that we take it back and move beyond employment as the sole pathway to social happiness. Living in a material hell is *not* enough to precipitate change: the dying embers of capitalism will not simply ignite a new world. Knowledge and critique are insufficient. "Without a credible and coherent alternative to capitalism," writes Fischer, "capitalist realism will continue to rule the political-economic unconscious."[15]

Setting Continents Ablaze

Desire, a primal force that ties humans and nonhumans, is a *rebellious* drive that can shatter "the interest of the dominated, exploited classes, and causes flows that are capable of . . . setting continents ablaze,"[16] according to Deleuze and Guattari. Faced with this energy, capitalism carefully and systematically codes desire around proto-fascist modes of living to ensure its survival: "social repression needs psychic repression precisely in order to form docile subjects and to ensure the reproduction of the social formation, including its repressive structures."[17] Across a range of social microinteractions, capitalism represses and arranges desire. "The truth is that sexuality is everywhere: the way a bureaucrat fondles his records, a judge administers justice, a businessman causes money to circulate; the way the bourgeoisie fucks the proletariat; and so on."[18]

13. Merrifield 2011, 160.
14. Santos 2014.
15. Fisher 2009, 78.
16. Deleuze and Guattari 2004, 115.
17. Deleuze and Guattari 2004, 127.
18. Deleuze and Guattari 2004, 322.

The shared intellect, the *intellectual commons,* is bombarded by capital. In the family, at home, at school, and at work, we are forced to repress the spontaneous, creative, and unpredictable energies of our desire. Social repression demands this ongoing psychic repression. However, this negative understanding is incomplete. Desire is always a *productive* force that manufactures the conditions for its *own* repression. In other words, while it is "of vital importance for a society to repress desire," write Deleuze and Guattari, capital goes a step further, "so that repression, hierarchy, exploitation, and servitude are themselves desired."[19] *We are made to desire our own repression.* People are not simply "duped" by ideological indoctrination: we learn to desire our repression. It is for this reason that desire functions without matching the (economic) interests of the subject. And why people continue to vote for politicians that eat them alive. As Deleuze ad Guattari write,

> That is why, when subjects, individuals, or groups act manifestly counter to their class interests . . . it is not enough to say: they were fooled, the masses have been fooled. It is not an ideological problem, a problem of failing to recognize, or of being subject to, an illusion. It is a problem of desire . . . unconscious investments are made according to positions of *desire* and uses of synthesis, very different from the interests of the subject, individual or collective, who desires.[20]

The existential problematic is how to *decode* and *redirect* desire beyond capitalist realism's repressive structures. Desire requires a new destination, an existential reorientation, what De Angelis terms a "destructive creation."[21] It is here that the imagination becomes important for painting a colorful world beyond the monochrome hues of the old. Capitalist realism saps the world of its magic, installing the oppressive fantasy of work-work-work, utterly deadening the human spirit. In the face of this dour reality that insists there is no alternative—our task is to redirect and unleash

---

19. Deleuze and Guattari 2004, 127.
20. Deleuze and Guattari 2004, 114.
21. De Angelis 2010.

desire beyond the fantasies of the global elite. The "good life," we are told, is impossible without a nine-to-five bullshit job.[22]

Our struggle is to free ourselves from this oppressive nightmare of grey cubicles, water coolers, bosses, and dream differently: not for more labor but for the reappropriation of the commons, the right to the world, and the right to an autonomous mode of existence. "Now," writes Merrifield, "the struggle is about taking back and redefining non-work life, about *everyday anti-capitalism and post-capitalist communality*."[23] The battle is rejecting work as labor, the meaning of work as labor, and a politics oriented exclusively by labor. As Merrifield adds, "figuring out practical alternatives to wage-labor, to time-wasting abstract labor, to empty time, and inventing a new economy that de-economizes exchange, frees up time, involves a new social configuration, and that reclaims space, is to threaten the capitalist system with *mass demobilization*."[24]

Challenging the exploitative idea of labor requires a long struggle against prevailing, hegemonic common sense. Antonio Gramsci wrote that common sense is the constellation of dominant views of social reality that articulates minds and bodies, thoughts and feelings, practices and habits, thereby rendering "alternatives to the 'common sense' as non-sense."[25] Common sense is more than just a cognitive state: it is not only what is *sensible* but what is *sensuous*— not only what we *think* but what we *feel*. Common sense is a form of sensuous commons: a shared pool of affects, emotions, and desires that disclose the *mood* of the world. It is therefore an important terrain of struggle.[26] By challenging common sense, we reconfigure the very conditions by which the impossible becomes possible, the unthought is thought, and the unfelt is felt. We don't have to wait for any leader to transform the existential conditions that we are immersed within—we are those conditions. We are the new-sense.

22. Graeber 2018.
23. Merrifield 2011, 19.
24. Merrifield 2011, 181.
25. Waterstone 2010, 882.
26. See Hall 1986.

The Right to the World

OUR EXISTENTIAL AUTONOMY—our dignity—depends on access, use, and ownership of the means of production, usually only attainable through the control of space and territory. This is something very different from receiving redistributed capital from the state (however important that lever is for basic survival). So long as there is inequality of space, and unequal access, society will embody tremendous misery. As Edward Soja argues, justice always-already has a *geography*[1]—and the equitable distribution of resources and services is a basic human right. Capitalist property relations, therefore, are an absolute obstacle to geographic justice. Property is impossible without accumulation by dispossession, and both are impossible without organized violence. Geographic justice, for us, is thus predicated on existential autonomy: the ability to produce, access, and share the spatial conditions of our existence—a new production of space to realize the promise of a dignified life for all. We now explore the co-constitutive roles of space and autonomy, as well as what Joe Nevins calls the "right to the world."[2] The right to the world, we argue, is a right to autonomous space. A right to the planet's commons in an age of brutal land acquisitions, ecological expulsions, rentierism, dispossession, and the warehousing of surplus humanity.

The Production of Space

Capitalism produces space. Armed with its generic blueprints, capital builds endless roads and railways, citadels of steel and

1. Soja 2010.
2. Nevins 2017.

glass, airports, shipping yards, austere government buildings, cookie-cutter houses, overscented shopping malls, military bases and battlefields, along with abandoned buildings, slums, prisons, poisoned rivers, plastic oceans, and toxic atmospheres. Every society is shaped by its surrounding space, and every space is shaped by its society.[3] Space is a social relation and, as such, a political relation. As Henri Lefebvre writes, "there is a politics of space because space is political."[4]

Capitalism organizes space and humanity according to the logic of accumulation. Its dreary landscapes appear apolitical, but they materialize logics of exploitation and control. "The spatial practice of the capitalist mode of production attempts to utilize instrumental space (space as a tool) and to institutionalize it, in order to introduce a coherence into exploitation and oppression, that is to say into the relations of production and class such as they are concretized 'on the ground,'"[5] writes Lefebvre. Capitalist space thus acquires the character of a violent class struggle—at the local, national, and *planetary scale*. It is what Lefebvre calls a "space of catastrophe" that "unsettles, atomizes, and pulverizes preexisting space, tearing it into pieces."[6] The fundamental contradiction is thus between *heterogenous* space-for-use (i.e., socialist space), and *homogenous* space-for-exchange (i.e., capitalist space). The struggle between a space for human flourishing and for capitalist accumulation is everywhere rampant and must be managed by the state: "the space of property cannot be established without its corollary: state space, which corrects and supports it."[7]

Our imaginations poisoned, and our autonomy stolen, many of us have ceded world-building to capitalism. Liberals repeatedly understand capital only through its deterritorialized circulation,

---

3. Lefebvre 1991.
4. Lefebvre 2009, 174.
5. Lefebvre 2009, 203.
6. Lefebvre 2009, 249.
7. Lefebvre 2009, 249; see also Parenti 2015.

failing to see its *production of space*. But as Lefebvre writes, "'To change life,' 'to change society,' these phrases mean nothing if there is no production of an appropriated space."[8] This is a most important lesson. There is no different mode of existence, no different world, no different politics, without a new production of space. As he adds, "The transformation of society presupposes a collective ownership and management of space."[9] In bourgeois thought, "justice" refers to the equitable distribution of things (such as money, or a universal basic income), and not to the equitable *production* of things—including, of course, the production of space.

Geographic justice, at its heart, uniquely insists on the equitable production of space. This territorial autonomy is fundamentally off-limits to capitalist realism (which may otherwise be willing to compromise on work conditions) and therefore presents a unique danger.

Autogestion

An autonomous production of space is what Lefebvre termed *autogestion*. This roughly translates as "self-management" or "worker control." It is "a radical attack on the foundations of capitalist social relations in which the bourgeoisie controls, through private ownership, the means of production."[10] Autogestion can be traced to the nineteenth century antistatist anarchist ideas of Pierre Joseph Proudhon,[11] to the classical liberal ideas of John Stuart Mill, and to twentieth century examples such as self-managed factories, including the Fiat Occupations in Turin and Milan in 1919–1920, Besancon, France, in 1973 and 2001, or Buenos Aires from 1971.[12] Lefebvre's hostility toward the state is inflected by

8. Lefebvre 2009, 186.
9. Lefebvre 1991, 422.
10. Purcell 2013, 147.
11. See Springer 2016 for more on anarchist geographies.
12. Purcell 2013.

his antipathy toward Stalinism. Actually existing "socialism" in the twentieth century had a very real problem of hypercentralization. Lefebvre thus builds on this tradition of factory occupations but widens the scope of autogestion to self-management in all areas of life. Autogestion is an autonomous production of space that opposes the capitalist and state mode of production. Autogestion is the class struggle written into space, "the site and the stake of struggle."[13] As Lefebvre argues,

> Each time a social group (generally the productive workers) refuses to accept passively its conditions of existence, of life, or of survival, each time a group forces itself not only to understand but to master its own conditions of existence, *autogestion* is occurring. This broad but precise definition shows *autogestion* to be a highly diversified practice that concerns businesses as well as territorial units, cities, and regions. This definition also includes all aspects of social life; it implies the strengthening of all associative ties, that is to say, of civil society. This theoretical definition points toward a practical struggle that is always reborn with failures and setbacks. Above all, this definition points to the fundamentally antistatist tendency of *autogestion*.[14]

Autogestion is a spatial struggle to occupy our "conditions of existence," or the landscapes of everyday life. Through a celebration of difference, spatial autonomy, and direct democracy, autogestion restores the primacy of use-values against commodity exchange. Revolution, so long as it is defined as political change at the level of state or capital, is necessarily incomplete. "Any revolutionary project today," writes Lefebvre, "whether utopian or realistic, must, if it is to avoid hopeless banality, make the reappropriation of the body, in association with the reappropriation of space, into a non-negotiable part of its agenda."[15] People must freely associate to appropriate their destiny. The state would not "wither away" overnight. But it would become increasingly unnecessary—no longer an arbitrator of the contradictions of everyday oppression.

13. Lefebvre 2009, 134.
14. Lefebvre 2009, 135.
15. Lefebvre 1991, 166–67.

The beating heart of Lefebvre's autogestion is the appropriation of space. Yet little of our contemporary politics, particularly in the global North, is *of* and *for* space.[16] Too often the state captures and polices space. Without the appropriation of space, we can only tinker with capitalism's circuits. Accordingly, Lefebvre writes that a society built on dignity, shared ownership, and use-value, must produce its own space. "The production of socialist space means the end of the private property and the state's political domination of space, which implies the passage from domination to appropriation and the primacy of use over exchange."[17] If capitalist space is a violent space of "quantification and growing homogeneity"; "a police space in which the state tolerates no resistance and no obstacles"; and one that strives for "the elimination of all differences," then "socialist space will be a space of differences."[18] Socialist space recognizes and produces difference. It protects a more autonomous mode of existence. And this right to autonomy, a right to a space of difference, poses an enormous threat to capitalism. Witness how even small spaces of autonomy and occupation have faced swift crackdown. In this regard the violent state reactions to the Occupy Movement (whose very name embodies these intentions) is instructive.[19]

The Right to the World

Lefebvre's socialist space is underpinned by what he first termed the "right to the city" in 1968. Under capitalism, our ability to reshape processes of urbanization, like all spatial processes, are severely constrained. Lefebvre's right to the city is a right for autonomous, publicly owned and managed urban spaces, and not simply the right of a neoliberal consumer. Accordingly, Harvey

16. Massey 2005.
17. Lefebvre 2009, 192.
18. Lefebvre 2009, 192.
19. Gitlin 2013.

argues that the right to the city "is a right to change ourselves by changing the city. It is, moreover, a common rather than an individual right since this transformation inevitably depends upon the exercise of a collective power to reshape the process of urbanization."[20] The right to the city has gained appeal in mainstream policy circles. Yet the radicality of a right to reshape our urban habitats has become diluted through its insertion into liberal-democratic frameworks.[21] Property rights, however, are an expropriation of urban space—an alienated form of rights that can be traded on the market place. For Lefebvre, as for Harvey, the right to the city means more than technocratic management. It is a struggle to remake the urban *beyond* capitalism.

Here, of course, we return to the concept of autogestion. Rights, for Lefebvre, are not "given" by the natural order, gods, or governments—they are won in social struggles. The right to autogestion is prominent for Lefebvre—a platform for revolutionary social change. Once everyone takes back control of their space, and desires autonomy over their "conditions of existence," state control is openly confronted. The right to the city is thus an explicitly spatial form of autogestion that aims to change the entirety of urban space and the urban way of life. As Purcell describes, "Lefebvre sees the right to the city as a struggle to 'de-alienate' urban space, to reintegrate it into the web of social connections. He talks about this de-alienation in terms of appropriation. His idea of the right to the city involves inhabitants appropriating space in the city."[22] The right to the city is a claim for autogestion—with residents uniting to manage the production of urban space for themselves. That is, "They are taking control of the conditions of their own existence. They are making the city their own again."[23]

20. Harvey 2008, 23.
21. Purcell 2013.
22. Purcell 2013, 149.
23. Purcell 2013, 150.

Beyond a right to the city: What about a right to the atmosphere, the biosphere, the lithosphere, the hydrosphere, and the technosphere? What if we take the right to autogestion to mean autonomy over our "conditions of existence" in its broadest, *planetary sense*? What if occupying the city is just one front in liberating the human condition? Here, we ask with Nevins, "What are the spatial conditions under which it is possible to be?"[24] Accordingly, what if we imagine a *right to the world,* a right to use, access, and occupy the fruits of the earth, of the commons—a right emblazoned across the banners of the dispossessed, the surplus, the paupers? Joe Nevins mobilizes the concept of the right to the world,[25] building upon Lefebvre's classic definition of the right to the city. But unlike a right that is rooted in a single space (and therefore privileges those within the city), the right to the world—which complements it and contains it—is characterized by a "right" to movement across the planet, and a share in its resources. This is a collective right in which those communities fleeing devastation—too often shipwrecked on hostile coasts—are guaranteed sanctuary. To deny, restrict, and police mobility in a world of uneven life and death chances is a denial of human rights. The right to the world is

> concerned with the individual (as well as collective) right to access global resources—among them, global space—so as to be able to realize the most basic of human rights: the right to a dignified life. But because this requires changing oneself and changing the world—not least by allowing for freedom of movement, residence, and work across national boundaries—it involves the exercise of collective power to reshape globalization and its associated spatialities.[26]

The right to the world transcends property rights, whether on a microscale, the scale of the city, or the scale of the nation-state. "In this regard, the right to the world entails a redefinition of the very concept of 'home' (as in homeland) so as to embrace Earth as

24. Nevins 2017, 1360.
25. Nevins 2017.
26. Nevins 2017, 1357.

the home of all humanity, one premised on human solidarity."[27] For us, the right to the world is a right to be able to live a dignified, safe, and above all *autonomous* existence—and that right is never complete but always an ongoing struggle for geographic justice.

27. Nevins 2017, 1362.

Alter-Worlds: A Manifesto

Alter-Worlds

We flourish, or we suffer, because of the world. With our first breath, we enter the world naked, vulnerable, and teetering on the edge of death. We depend entirely on the world for our survival. For months and years afterward, we exist *only* because we coexist. Our little lives are folded into the past sacrifices of nameless others. "Whether or not we acknowledge it," writes Gibson-Graham, "our own existence at every level can be seen as the effect of the labor of others."[1] The human condition and the world are forever one. Human beings, writes Arendt, "are not just in the world they are of the world."[2] Worlds are the ecosystems of our coexistence: composed of other people, plants, rivers, infrastructures, the rich tapestry of shared being. Yet we are soon told we are *individuals*. Beaten down into lonely atoms. For the Invisible Committee, "Two centuries of capitalist and market nihilism have brought us the most extreme alienations— from our selves, from others, from worlds."[3] Our task is to rethink, reclaim, rebuild, beyond our alienated worlds.

The foundational world-alienation is the onset of a universal space-time. It is the idea of *a* world that is so oppressive. As the Zapatistas stated in their 1996 declaration, "In the world we want many worlds to fit." The originary disaster of capitalism was the ravaging of all incompatible worlds.[4] "All that now persists is an eternal present," writes Merrifield, "a contaminated present, a repressive situation accepted as a perfectly natural reality, as the

---

1. Gibson-Graham 2006, 88.
2. Arendt 1971, 20.
3. The Invisible Committee 2009, 8.
4. The Invisible Committee 2009, 30.

only reality."[5] Capitalism installs a singular, undifferentiated, global space of exchange—and violently subjugates other worlds. Not only are alternative worlds needed desperately now, but they *are* possible. The Zapatistas seized space, time, and value from capitalist realism—asserting an autonomous mode of existence and calendar. The alternative worlds, or alter-worlds, we describe, blossom from singularity within plurality. The challenge, writes Roelvink, is "to expand the focus on dignified workers to also consider a dignified world."[6]

We now find ourselves in a world sculpted by capital's image—but with little place left for us. The *lumpen* face new modes of biopolitical division, apartheid, and exterminism. So why continue to *only* modify the toxic political economy of the present regime? Since so many of the planet's surplus populations now live on the outside of a shrinking capitalist interior, this presents an opportunity as much as it does a disaster. Accordingly, our insistence on building alter-worlds stems from our desire to escape the black hole of capitalist realism entirely: to produce and occupy commons animated by shared means of existence. A revitalized politics cannot be content with wealth redistribution without geographic justice. Alter-worlds are decommodified and autonomous territories: entangled spaces of being, of unique stories-so-far, of dignified coexistence between humans and nonhumans. Alter-worlds render capital, rather than humanity, surplus to requirement. So long as what Lefebvre calls the "conditions of existence" are in private hands, human lives will remain disposable.

We need a new production of space. We must imagine, design, desire, build, rebuild, celebrate, paint, and story alter-worlds. We must supplant centuries of capitalist worldlessness with new landscapes of dignity for all. For there can be no existential autonomy without spatial autonomy. Both Lefebvre and the Zapatistas articulate this

5. Merrifield 2011, 13.
6. Roelvink 2016, 150.

point. An alter-world is an autonomous *spatial machine*: made of interlocking parts, spaces, flows, humans, gears, rivers, airs, roads, animals, seeds, electricity. And it is alive: with humans and other animals working the land, and the land working both. Alter-worlds enable us to exercise autonomy, celebrate liberty, reclaim and protect our communities, and enjoy the pleasure of simple human dignity. An alter-world is not just a space-time or a location on a map: it is also a mode of existence, a way of being-in-the-world. Alter-worlds are alternative geographies to capitalist realism and its toxic subjectifications—they are autonomous territories where people freely associate to work, live, and care for each other.

The battle is for the very contours of the world, not just the factory or the workplace. As Gorz writes, "Autonomy in work is of little significance when it is not carried into the cultural, moral, and political spheres."[7] Temporary and permanent autonomous zones, worker's councils, community gardens, free schools, pirate radio stations, squats, collectives, communes, LETs, and other parallel institutions are all important spaces for refuge and prefiguring new postcapitalist politics. The beating heart of alter-worlds is the appropriation of the commons. As Gibson-Graham writes, community economies enable, "creating, enlarging, reclaiming, replenishing, and sharing a commons, acknowledging the interdependence of individuals, groups, nature, things, traditions, and knowledges, and tending the commons as a way of tending the community."[8] But without spatial autonomy, the status of any community economy is precarious.

The commons are fields of corn, neighborhood libraries, rivers, museums, parks, woodlands, beaches, forests, oceans, schools, knowledges, livelihoods, cognitive capacities. All these enrich the quality of our lives—offsetting inequality and providing spaces of social cohesion.[9] Yet these natural and social fruits of the earth

7. Gorz 1999, 40.
8. Gibson-Graham 2006.
9. Venn 2018, 119–20.

are under constant attack by capital's great war of enclosure. The *disembedding* of the world prevented humans from surviving on and *with* the land. For the Invisible Committee, "The destruction of the peasant's world and of local alimentary practices meant the disappearance of the means for dealing with scarcity."[10] Our call is not for a return to a lost rustic past, but a demand for an autonomous, dignified future for the billions denied existential freedoms in the singular unworld of capital. Such a pathway forward could be called a neo-peasant ontology. Reclaiming the art and skills of the "peasants world" signals a livelihood based *with* the earth and connects to the many peasants in the global South today. What do we learn by imagining a neo-peasant ontology?

Capital destroyed multiple existential strategies in which humans associated as *beings-with*. These, to recall Polanyi, were *householding* (or *autarky*), *reciprocity,* and *redistribution*. Together, they provide us with the keystones for alter-worlds and autonomous territorial existence. *Householding,* as Polanyi argues, was a form of production for the satisfaction of an individual's or community's immediate need—not production for exchange or gain on the market. *Reciprocity* is a form of mutual aid and gift exchange embedded in kinship and instituted across communities. *Redistribution* is the allocation and sharing of resources based on community need (organized, historically, by a center, such as a tribal chief). Our cosmology for alter-worlds pivots around these three stars: autarky, reciprocity, and redistribution. Alter-worlds embed human economic activity *within* the immanent needs and interests of local communities. For Polanyi, "Those interests will be very different in a small hunting or fishing community from those in a vast despotic society, but in either case the economic system will be run on noneconomic motives."[11]

Alter-worlds are driven by the principle of social use-value. We must substitute the entrenched motivation for economic gain

10. The Invisible Committee 2009, 53.
11. Polanyi 2001, 48.

with subsistence (richly and expansively defined). Economies must serve social organizations. Alter-worlds, we must emphasize, however, are not a step backward, but a step sideways. Nor are they necessarily small. As Polanyi insists, "It should by no means be inferred that socioeconomic principles of this type are restricted to primitive procedures or small communities; that a gainless and marketless economy must necessarily be simple."[12] There are various technologies that could perform worldly autonomy on larger scales, including advances in solar, wind, and other forms of renewable energies. There are already multiple examples across the planet of communities going "off the grid" (as well as those illustrated above in section 7, who have never been "on the grid"). As Venn writes, our task "should be inventing new methods for producing food and the necessities of life, for instance, by deploying energy technologies based on ambient energy sources."[13] This form of high-tech autonomy can be performed at a scale that *widens* with social organization. *Solar peasants!*

We urgently require new infrastructures to repair our fragile spheres of coexistence that multiple communities can plug into. The backbone of alter-worlds is communal infrastructure. Infrastructure, writes Berlant, is "the lifeworld of structure. Roads, bridges, schools, food chains, finance systems, prisons, families, districts, norms all the systems that link ongoing proximity to being in a world-sustaining relation."[14] Today, so much of our shared, worldly infrastructure stands in ruin, is privatized, and there is little desire left to rebuild. "Mid-twentieth century forms of expansive world building toward the good life have little or unreliable traction."[15] Yet rebuilding infrastructural commons *transforms common sense*. Shared power grids, internet structures, green energies, and clean technologies, each perform different worldings of common sense.

12. Polanyi 2001, 52.
13. Venn 2018, 17.
14. Berlant 2016, 393.
15. Berlant 2016, 409.

Locating a single space that contains an alter-world is difficult, for they cannot be captured easily by static maps. There are examples, such as the Zapatistas in Chiapas, with more explicitly bordered autonomous territories. But for most of the planet (as we illustrate above), the battle will be spatially complex and involve stitching together disparate sites of potential. At the beginning, the roots of alter-worlds are rhizomatic: tunnels, passages, exits, and entrances in the flesh of the planet, where commoners gather and disperse. Abandoned buildings, community gardens, volunteer centers, online commons, lakes and seas that connect nations, each serve as sites of potential new-sense and relational connections. In the zombiescapes of capital, we find microspaces of sanctuary and rebirth.

Alter-Work

Waged work was won in the blood, mud, and tears of the great war of enclosure, leaving a landless working class with "nothing to sell except their own skins"[16] for Marx. Accordingly, we need to be careful with how we use the term *work*—since its definition affects how we imagine future worlds. Under capitalism, work is typically servile in nature: we sell our time—our existence on planet Earth—to somebody else, leading to a global division between those who sell their time and those who buy it. And most bullshit jobs gift nothing to the world.[17] Work must be *reclaimed* and *reworlded* from capital. Our task is to build, craft, sew, engineer, cook, fix, grow, plumb our way to more dignified worlds. This is no small task. We've forgotten how to build, and under the spell of capitalist realism, we've *forgotten that we've forgotten*. For generations, humanity has been stripped of its worldly skills and autonomous capacities. Our call is for a shift from a vision of work oriented by

16. Marx 1990, 873.
17. Graeber 2018.

capitalist laboring—of *jobs, jobs, jobs* (one that is ever more mean-ingless on a planet of wageless life)—to a vision of work directed at resourcing alter-worlds.

So much of our daily activity is not directed at the world. It is either indifferent, or hostile, to the plural conditions of our more-than-human coexistence. In the wake of the industrial revolution—and European colonialism—work shifted from pro-tecting our worldly, existential autonomy to selling ourselves to somebody else under conditions of duress. The existential trifold of householding *(autarky)*, reciprocity *(mutual aid)*, and redistri-bution *(sharing)* was attacked by capital's system of enclosure, waged and divided labor, and slavery. As Gorz puts it, "The eco-nomic rationalization of work will thus sweep away the ancient idea of freedom and existential autonomy. It produces individuals who, being alienated in their work, will, necessarily, be alienated in their consumption as well and, eventually, in their needs."[18] The great transformation changed the human condition. Instead of producing for ourselves, our communities, and our ecologies, we became individuals forced to labor for the owner of our labor pow-er, and "for whom the essential objective of work is to earn enough to buy commodities."[19] From *working for the world* to *laboring for a boss*. We woke up, as the Invisible Committee perfectly sums up, in "a world where 'becoming self-sufficient' is a euphemism for 'having found a boss.'"[20]

The *alter-work* we describe nurtures postcapitalist existence by emphasizing autonomous, de-alienated, work. We find much val-ue in Arendt's distinction between the human activities of *work* and *labor*. Work, Arendt writes, is an ancient *world-building* craft. Work creates durable objects that nourish, strengthen, and main-tain public worlds. This understanding of human activity is what Arendt calls *Homo faber* ("human the maker"). *Homo faber* is an

18. Gorz 1989, 22.
19. Gorz 1989, 22.
20. The Invisible Committee 2009, 26.

existential engineer—a builder of worlds. For millennia, *Homo faber* crafted artifacts to nourish and strengthen the world. The sum total of these objects formed what Arendt terms the artifice: a *common infrastructure* of worldly structures to shelter us.[21] Without this infrastructure, we are left exposed to the endless cycles of commodified life, "the deathless everlastingness of the human as of all other species."[22] Without work, which is worldliness, all that's left is the naked circulation of capital.

The ancient worldly practice of work came under attack with capitalist relations of production. Autonomous spatial activities were relentlessly enclosed. The human species was forced to *labor* for someone else, and the production of commodities did little to strengthen the world. The working classes were deskilled and reduced to their biological survivalism: becoming *animal laborans,* the laboring animal. Laboring has always existed. But the great transformation elevated it above worldly work to the mythical and oppressive status it now occupies above all others. Again, as the Invisible Committee write, "The horror of work is less in the work itself than in the methodical ravaging, for centuries, of all that isn't work: the familiarities of one's neighborhood and trade, of one's village, of struggle, of kinship, our attachment to places, to beings, to the seasons, to ways of doing and speaking."[23] Laboring-for-consumption came to occupy the means and ends of human activity. And the world suffered, as the perishable commodity became the organizing principle for life on earth.

We want to recover Arendt's meaning of work in our conception of alter-work: autonomous world-making activity that supports common coexistence. This form of decommodified activity is directed at resourcing, repairing, and rebuilding the world. While this type of work once defined the human condition, as *Homo faber,* today it is much rarer. Our challenge is thus to *work* for alter-worlds:

21. Arendt 2013, 136.
22. Arendt 2013, 97.
23. The Invisible Committee 2009, 30.

whether we perform this activity at food banks, fabric banks, book banks, shared kitchens, community documentaries, river restoration projects, community gardens, cooperatives, street parties, music workshops, housebuilding, autonomous schools and universities, or a multitude of (socialist) spaces directed by use-value. Freedom and happiness flourish when everyday life is composed *less* of laboring for another, and more time spent working for, and simply enjoying, the world. Alter-work moves ever outwards: from the individual, to the house, the street, the neighborhood, the village, extending to the horizons of entirely new worlds. For Gorz, "It can *open up* the private sphere on to a space of *common sovereignty,* shielded from commodity relations, where individuals *together* determine for themselves their common needs, and decide the most appropriate actions for satisfying them."[24] Local communities become incubators for alter-worlds to "protect individuals from becoming isolated, lonely, and withdrawn."[25]

Unless we take ownership of our own work, our ability to *exteriorize* ourselves—to realize our existential autonomy—is limited. As Arendt defines the tragedy of our situation: "What we are confronted with is the prospect of a society of laborers without labor, that is, without the only activity left to them. Surely, nothing could be worse."[26] Unlike laboring, alter-work enables people to inscribe their existence into the flesh of the world. This, writes Gorz, is a process of "exteriorization by which subjects achieve self-realization by inscribing themselves upon the objective materiality of what they create or produce."[27] Alter-work is *building* and *reshaping* the contours of our shared reality. Alter-work produces novel foldings of matter and thought, new architectures of being, through the free association of people, rivers, objects, solar panels, fish, corn, dams, robots, houses, windmills—the colorful geography of being.

24. Gorz 1989, 159–60.
25. Gorz 1989, 159.
26. Arendt 2013, 5.
27. Gorz 1999, 2.

When one builds, when one fabricates, one brings into the world something that didn't exist before—it is a moment of realization and of potential. So much anger, sadness, and despair comes from having so little invested—so little inscribed—in our surrounding environment. The worlds that many of us labor in provide neither a space of exteriorization nor of nourishment. The surfaces and depths of capitalism's unworld are *enclosed,* off-limits, secured, surveilled—and utterly indifferent to our existence.

Alter-work strives to leave the world a better, more dignified, more loving place. We do this work all the time. *But we must reclaim it as our own.* This requires seizing our autonomy back: reclaiming enclosed land—from the abandoned urban park to the ancient commons contaminated by capital's waste. For too long, capital has *deskilled* vast swathes of the planet, reducing us to hyperactive zombies. This reaches its most violent endpoint with the automated economy. A surplus population that cannot plant, that cannot craft, that cannot learn, cannot engineer alter-worlds. Grow. Dream. Build.

> It's a question of knowing how to fight, to pick locks, to set broken bones and treat sickness; how to build a pirate radio transmitter; how to set up street kitchens; how to aim straight; how to gather together scattered knowledge and set up wartime agronomics; understand plankton biology; soil composition; study the ways plants interact; get to know possible uses for and connections with our immediate environment as well as the limits we can't go beyond without exhausting it.[28]

Alter-Politics

What is freedom? Freedom is spatial autonomy. Communal coexistence. The kind of deep, ontological security, that flows from controlling the shared conditions of existence. "Freedom consists . . . in reconquering spaces of autonomy in which we can *will what we*

---

28. The Invisible Committee 2009, 71.

are doing and take responsibility for it," writes Gorz.[29] So much of our political imagination is based on the hierarchies (managers, bosses, leaders) of capitalism—rather than free and equal access to the commons. The politicians of capitalist realism fight to preserve its resplendent horror: *you must work, even when you cannot work*! There are cracks in the system and plenty of politicians that do care. But for the most part, politics is reduced to an economic question of who dominates whom. Alter-politics, conversely, seeks to reclaim shared access and ownership of the commons. It does not seek to compel surplus populations back into capitalist society. Nor does it seek to install a dictatorship of the proletariat. An alter-politics, write Hardt and Negri, has "nothing to do with full employment or giving everyone a job; rather it has to do with fostering the expansion of our powers to think and create, to generate images and social relationships, to communicate and cooperate."[30]

Alter-politics is the call, the demand, and the practice of spatial justice. Wherever we find ourselves, our political task is to assemble and work for the world. Such a "progressive localism"[31] calls for us to support new spaces of coexistence and recognize those that already exist. These incipient, fragile worlds are bubbling across the planet. And they require us—whether students, teachers, academics, activists, artists, gardeners, architects, or builders—to resource them. But how do we mobilize those wasted lives who have zero investment in a system that has zero investment in them? As Hardt and Negri put it, the "challenge will be to find ways to translate the productivity and possibility of the poor into power."[32] The latent power of surplus populations is not—as with the traditional working classes—a negative power to *withhold* their labor. Instead, alter-politics is a *positive power* to build alterworlds inside and outside the singular unworld of capital. This is

29. Gorz 1989, 166.
30. Hardt and Negri 2009, 299.
31. Featherstone et al. 2012.
32. Hardt and Negri 2009, xi.

a politics of *existential fabrication*. It is a politics performed by the skills of the poor, the destitute, the surplus, to begin anew. The repeated failure of mainstream politics can, in part, be attributed to its necessary and willful failure to recognize—and celebrate—the human as *Homo faber*. In this sense, alter-politics does not gather traditional working-class identities. Alter-politics is lodged in the open condition of being-poor-in-the-world, of virtual pauperhood, of worldlessness, rather than the abstract, staged, politics of capitalist realism. Being poor, after all, is a democratic category: "a radically plural and open body politic."[33]

The struggle is also inwards. We cannot change the world without changing ourselves. "When all is said and done, it's with an entire anthropology that we are at war."[34] We must lose our selves to discover who we can be. But subjective change is so difficult because of the immense desire people invest in the deadening repetitions of capitalism. "The process of disclosing new worlds," writes Gibson-Graham, "involves complex movements between identification with new subject positions, exploratory acts of self-transformation."[35] We live in a system that prizes the most psychotic impulses of humanity: greed, violence, and reckless individualism. Alter-politics works tirelessly to undo this psychic damage. It replaces the closed, lonely figure of the human—the master of the universe—with a fundamentally *open* being that is immersed within symbiotic relationships. *A strength that comes from fragility*. Human being, in other words, as *being-with*: an epigenetic creature of the world. Being-with-rivers, being-with-plants, being-with-tools, being-with-crops, being-with-skies, being-with-others. As Jean-Luc Nancy writes,

> Being cannot *be* anything but being-with-one-another, circulating in the *with* and as the *with* of this singularly plural coexistence. . . . But this circulation goes in all directions at once, in all the directions of

33. Hardt and Negri 2009, 39
34. The Invisible Committee 2009, 8.
35. Gibson-Graham 2006, 162.

all the space-times opened by presence to presence: all things, all beings, all entities, everything past and future, alive, dead, inanimate, stones, plants, nails, gods—and "humans," that is, all those who expose sharing and circulation as such by saying "we."[36]

Our existence is coexistence. Being open with the world is a source of strength. We must move from the toxic divisions installed by capitalism toward a reciprocal understanding of our bonds within the web of life. The victory of *animal laborans* over *Homo faber* entrenched a politics of domination: humans were stuffed into factories, and animals into factory farms. We must open ourselves to the joy and suffering of others. Alter-politics is at war with atomization, massification, and the generic, consumable politics of capital. For too long we've been deworlded and reduced to isolated particles. Capitalist realism thrives on producing docile subjects who are alienated from their surroundings. Alter-politics fights for new worlds for new people, and new people for new worlds. We must restore the link between self and world so that it is not an estranged, managerial relationship of domination. We must recognize our fundamental being as "creatures among creatures, singularities among similars, living flesh weaving the flesh of the world."[37] Alter-politics recognizes that dignified worlds depend on treating nonhumans with dignity, and understands our symbiotic, complex, and fragile nature with the earth.

Private property, backed by the law, is a big obstacle to commoning. This is what Hardt and Negri term the *republic of property,* which encloses "the conditions of possibility of social life in all its facets and phases."[38] Yet the "multitude of the poor presents an objective menace to the republic of property."[39] Accordingly, Hardt and Negri call for an *alter-modernity* that is based on a renewed idea of communism. This is different from either capitalism

36. Nancy 2000, 3.
37. The Invisible Committee 2009, 20–21.
38. Hardt and Negri 2009, 8.
39. Hardt and Negri, 2009, 45.

or socialism. Both, write Hardt and Negri, are "regimes of property that exclude the common. The political project of instituting the common . . . cuts across these false alternatives—neither private nor public, neither capitalist nor socialist—and opens new spaces for politics."[40] Their alter-modernity, as with the Zapatistas, "orients the forces of resistance more clearly toward an autonomous terrain."[41] As they add, "we could begin to define communism this way: what the private is to capitalism and what the public is to socialism, the common is to communism."[42] Communism, rather than a dictatorship, a state, or a party, is an idea that—for the Invisible Committee—names "all worlds resisting imperial pacification, all solidarities irreducible to the reign of commodities."[43]

We understand poverty not simply as a lack of a (waged) job but, more fundamentally, as a lack of access to the earth, as a denied *right to the world*. Alter-worlds, alter-work, alter-politics: placing power in the resourcefulness of people. Instead of fighting over capitalist space, we must build autonomous spaces. Instead of fighting over capitalist jobs, we must work for the world. Instead of fighting over capitalist politics, we must fight for the commons. We need to find each other and assemble. Resource those imaginations that dream differently. Support each other. We need to become apprentices of the world and learn from our neighbors: the peasants, doctors, grandparents, engineers, and paupers. Study. Love each other. Become *planetologists*. As Subcomandante Galeano writes, "If no geographic locations exist for that tomorrow, we start gathering twigs, stones, strips of clothing, meat, bones, and clay. We begin constructing an island, or better yet, a rowboat, that we plant in the middle of tomorrow, where one can still just barely see the storm looming ahead."[44]

40. Hardt and Negri 2009, ix.

41. Hardt and Negri 2009, 102.

42. Hardt and Negri 2009, 273.

43. The Invisible Committee 2009, 8; see also Badiou 2008; Swyngedouw 2009.

44. Galeano 2015, 167.

Last Thoughts: The Alienated

A SPECTER IS HAUNTING THE WORLD. It is wageless life. The struggle Marx articulated rested on workers in industrializing Europe. Today, it falls on capitalism's billions of surplus lives. The future will not be dictated by those with waged work. For better or worse, it is in the hands of the outcast. The poor, write Hardt and Negri, are no longer on the geographic borders of capitalism "but increasingly at its heart—and thus the multitude of the poor emerges also at the center of the project for revolutionary transformation."[1] For now, at least, the one percent are safe in their underground bunkers. But no matter how deep they entomb their wealth, nobody can hide from a world on fire. Pauperism befalls armies of workers in the middle classes. Good people, accustomed to comfort, peer out the windows of their suburban homes, staring at the storm darkening their little worlds. Dial 911. Capitalism is choking to death.

The coming storm is already creating a frenzied mess of our politics. State leaders, some of them wearing fascist red caps, swing between punishing the poor and promising more jobs. We support higher wages for workers. But this is not enough, especially in the new Dark Age. Marx was clear on this: "A forcing up of wages . . . would therefore be nothing but better payment for the slave, and would not conquer either for the worker or for labor their human status and dignity."[2] As he immediately adds, "Wages are a direct consequence of estranged labor, and estranged labor is the direct cause of private property. The downfall of one aspect must there-

1. Hardt and Negri 2009, 86.
2. Marx 1988, 81–82.

fore involve the downfall of the other." Wages and private property spawn from the same terror: the great war of enclosure. Many
of us now live in a world of private property but no wages. The
horror of capital has been stripped to its most naked expression.
Our political imagination is radically truncated if we see the ane-
mic welfare state or the desire for a waged life as the only shelters
from the coming storm. Human liberty, equality, and dignity are
realized only by free access to the commons.

The alienated are legion: their ranks now swelling with the middle classes. Marx describes the proletariat as a class that "has a universal character because of its universal suffering."[3] But the common
understanding of the proletariat is limited. Instead, we insist the
proletarian is a *virtual pauper*: the central figure of alienation that
is always becoming surplus to capital. This worldless pauper, with
no home, no job, no security, now exists in staggering numbers. It
presents a menace to both capitalism and human dignity. A war of
all against all is a very *real* future of capitalism. Wageless life contains both a destructive and creative potential. Everything depends
on whether we can build alter-worlds in the wastelands of the old
regime—and we can only guess how the global elite will react to
the coming storm. Harvey warns that capitalism's survival could
be violently extended, despite the wretched conditions:

> It could do so, for example, by a capitalist oligarchic elite supervis-
> ing the mass genocidal elimination of much of the world's surplus
> and disposable population while enslaving the rest and building vast
> artificial gated communities to protect against the ravages of an ex-
> ternal nature run toxic, barren, and ruinously wild. Dystopian tales
> abound depicting a grand variety of such worlds and it would be
> wrong to rule them out as impossible blueprints for the future of a
> less-than-human humanity.[4]

Alienation is an important rallying cry to challenge the economic and existential oppression of capitalism. *We, the many virtual*

---

3. Marx 1975, 256
4. Harvey 2014, 246.

and actual paupers, are each born surplus to requirement, worldless in an enclosed planet, and *dispossessed in a regime of possession.* Our unique singularity, from the perspective of capital, was— and is—irrelevant. Alienation, as a concept and platform for political change, holds radical potential by politicizing the terrible indignities of poverty, the traumas of depression, and the terror of structural violence. Alienation is felt in the immediate cruelties of capitalism: it gathers the best and the worst of us across the complex geographies of capitalism. We must advance our politics away from an economic framing of poverty and toward the existential condition of worldlessness. Even in the most depraved conditions we find hope. For Bloch, "The zero point of the most extreme alienation, as represented by the proletariat, ultimately becomes the point of dialectical reversal. Within the nothingness of this zero point, Marx teaches, we may find our whole world."[5] It's either that or barbarism!

We must fight for a whole new world. We are the world, after all. In its darkest depths and most jagged peaks, we realize our species-being. "Just as plants, animals, stones, air, light, etc., constitute theoretically a part of human consciousness . . . so also in the realm of practice they constitute a part of human life and human activity," wrote Marx.[6] City or farm, soil or concrete, appropriating space has never been more essential for our survival. The alter-worlds we have articulated seek to nurture species-being by creating a dignified geography of existence. As more of us join the swelling ranks of the planet's surplus populations—perhaps our commonalities as virtual paupers will unite us in the face of violent efforts to divide us. But there is a big source of uncertainty: the act of letting go. The existential leap of faith. Paulo Freire termed the "fear of freedom" our preference for even apparent security over the risk of freedom. As he writes, "the oppressed,

5. Bloch 2018, 21.
6. Marx 1988, 75

who have adapted to the structure of domination in which they are immersed, and have become resigned to it, are inhibited from waging the struggle for freedom so long as they feel incapable of running the risks it requires."[7]

Wherever we find ourselves, we each have a right to the world. Buried beneath the skeletons of capital's war of enclosure lies this truth. But the right to the world will never be given—only taken back. And time is running out, for the storm is already here, howling and wheezing, the miserable death rattle of capitalism fills the skies. No matter. We must march on, against the wind and rain, tossed between rubble and ruin, for the simple love of the world.

We will make it easier to imagine the end of capitalism than the end of our world. *Paupers of the world, unite!*

7. Freire 2007, 47–48.

Acknowledgments

This project began with a multiyear graduate student reading group focused on the deepening, myriad crises of late stage capitalism, particularly the growing numbers of "surplus" people. Marv is grateful for the diligence and curiosity of those scholars, and especially to the most persistent of them, his coauthor Ian Shaw. Marv would like to thank his wife, Penny, who is patiently accommodating his enduring misunderstanding of the concept of "retirement." Second, Ian would like to acknowledge the University of Minnesota Press and the University of Glasgow, and to all those in his life who supported the book. Ian would also like to thank Marv Waterstone, Sallie Marston, and JP Jones, for years of friendship and mentorship (and particularly Marv for all the Marx reading groups!). Finally, the project benefited from the insightful and careful attention of two reviewers, whose comments and suggestions improved our initial efforts.

Works Cited

Alves, Jaime Amparo. 2014. "From Necropolis to Blackpolis: Necropolitical Governance and Black Spatial Praxis in São Paulo, Brazil." *Antipode* 46, no. 2: 323–39.

Araujo, Erin. 2017. "Resource-Full Organized Communities Undermine Systems of Domination: How the Poor Rise Up in San Cristobal de las Casas." In *Why Don't the Poor Rise Up? Organizing the Twenty-First Century Resistance,* ed. Ajamu Nangwaya and Michael Truscello, 199–212. Chico, Calif.: AK Press.

Arendt, Hannah. 1971. *The Life of the Mind.* New York: Houghton Mifflin Harcourt.

Arendt, Hannah. 2013. *The Human Condition.* Chicago: University of Chicago Press.

Badiou, Alain. 2008. "The Communist Hypothesis." *New Left Review* 49:29–42.

Baptist, Edward E. 2014. *The Half Has Never Been Told: Slavery and the Making of American Capitalism.* New York: Basic Books.

Bauman, Zygmunt. 2004. *Wasted Lives: Modernity and Its Outcasts.* Cambridge, UK: Polity Press.

Berlant, Lauren. 2011. *Cruel Optimism.* Durham, N.C.: Duke University Press.

Berlant, Lauren. 2016. "The Commons: Infrastructures for Troubling Times." *Environment and Planning D: Society and Space* 34, no. 3: 393–419.

Blakeley, Grace. 2019. *Stolen: How to Save the World from Financialisation.* London: Repeater Books.

Bloch, Ernst. 2018. *On Karl Marx.* Trans. John Maxwell. London: Verso.

Breman, J. 2016. *On Pauperism in Present and Past.* Oxford: Oxford University Press.

Buckley, Michelle. 2013. "Locating Neoliberalism in Dubai: Migrant Workers and Class Struggle in the Autocratic City." *Antipode* 45, no. 2: 256–74.

Chatterton, Paul. 2010. "Autonomy: The Struggle for Survival, Self-Management, and the Common; Introduction." *Antipode* 42, no. 4: 897–908.

Chen, Martha, Chris Bonner, and Françoise Carré. 2015. *Organizing Informal Workers: Benefits, Challenges, and Successes.* New York:

United Nations Development Program. Final Report available at: http://hdr.undp.org/sites/default/files/chen_hdr_2015_final.pdf.

Choplin, Armelle, and Riccardo Ciavolella. 2017. "Gramsci and the African Città Futura: Urban Subaltern Politics from the Margins of Nouakchott, Mauritania." *Antipode* 49, no. 2: 314–34.

Collins, Randall. 2013. "The End of Middle-Class Work: No More Escapes." In *Does Capitalism Have a Future?* ed. Immanuel Wallerstein, Randall Collins, Michael Mann, Georgi Derluguian, and Craig Calhoun, 37–70. Oxford: Oxford University Press.

Cowen, Deborah, and Amy Siciliano. 2011. "Surplus Masculinities and Security." *Antipode* 43, no. 5: 1516–41.

Davis, Mike. 2004. "Planet of Slums: Urban Involution and the Informal Proletariat." *New Left Review* 26 (March/April): 5–34.

Davis, Mike. 2006. *Planet of Slums*. London: Verso.

De Angelis, M. 2010. "The Production of Commons and the 'Explosion of the Middle Class.'" *Antipode* 42, no. 4: 954–77.

de Certeau, Michel. 1984. *The Practice of Everyday Life*. Trans. Steven F. Rendall. Berkeley: University of California Press.

Deleuze, Gilles, and Félix Guattari. 2004. *Anti-Oedipus*. Trans. Brian Masumi. London: Continuum.

Denning, M. 2010. "Wageless Life." *New Left Review* 66 (November/December): 79–98.

Engels, Friedrich. 2009. *The Condition of the Working-Class in England*. Oxford: Oxford University Press.

Engels, Friedrich. 1972. *The Origin of the Family, Private Property, and the State*. New York: Pathfinder Press.

Engels, Friedrich. 2016. *The Peasant War in Germany*. Full text available at: https://www.marxists.org/archive/marx/works/1850/peasant-war -germany/index.htm.

Evans, Brad, and Zygmunt Bauman. 2016. "The Refugee Crisis Is Humanity's Crisis." *New York Times,* May 2, 2016. https://www .nytimes.com/2016/05/02/opinion/the-refugee-crisis-is-humanitys -crisis.html.

Fairlie, Simon. 2009. "A Short History of Enclosure in Britain." *The Land*. http://www.thelandmagazine.org.uk/articles/short-history-enclosure -britain.

Fanon, Frantz. 1963. *The Wretched of the Earth*. Trans. Richard Philcox. New York: Grove Press.

Featherstone, D., Anthony Ince., Danny Mackinnon, Kendra Strauss, and Andy Cumbers. 2012. "Progressive Localism and the Construction of Political Alternatives." *Transactions of the Institute of British Geographers* 37, no. 2: 177–82.

Fernandez, Bina. 2018. "Dispossession and the Depletion of Social Reproduction." *Antipode* 50, no. 1: 142–63.

Fisher, Mark. 2009. *Capitalist Realism: Is There No Alternative?* Winchester, UK: 0 Books.

Frase, Peter. 2016. *Four Futures: Visions of the World after Capitalism.* London: Verso.

Freeman, Richard. 2015. "Who Owns the Robots Rules the World." *IZA World of Labor,* May: 1–10.

Foucault, Michel. 2003. *"Society Must Be Defended": Lectures at the Collège de France, 1975–1976.* Trans. David Macey. New York: Penguin.

Freire, Paulo. 2007. *Pedagogy of the Oppressed.* New York: Continuum.

Frey, Carl B., and Michael A. Osborne. 2013. "The Future of Employment: How Susceptible Are Jobs to Computerisation?" September 17, 2013. https://www.oxfordmartin.ox.ac.uk/downloads/academic/The _Future_of_Employment.pdf.

Frey, Carl B., Thor Berger, and Chinchih Chen. 2018. "Political Machinery: Did Robots Swing the 2016 US Presidential Election?" *Oxford Review of Economic Policy* 34, no. 3: 418–42.

Galeano, Subcomandante. 2016. *Sixth Commission of the Zapatista Army for National Liberation. Critical Thoughts in the Face of the Capitalist Hydra I.* Durham, N.C.: Paperboat Press.

Gibson-Graham, J. K. 2006. *The End of Capitalism (As We Knew It): A Feminist Critique of Political Economy.* Minneapolis: University of Minnesota Press.

Gidwani, Vinay, and Rajyashree N. Reddy. 2011. "The Afterlives of 'Waste': Notes from India for a Minor History of Capitalist Surplus." *Antipode* 43, 5: 1625–58.

Gilmore, Ruth W. 2007. *Golden Gulag: Prisons, Surplus, Crisis, and Opposition in Globalizing California.* Berkeley: University of California Press.

Giroux, Henry. A. 2002. "Global Capitalism and the Return of the Garrison State: Rethinking Hope in the Age of Insecurity." *Arena Journal* 19 (Fall 2002): 141–60.

Gitlin, Todd. 2013. "What the Occupy Wall Street Crackdown Can Teach Us about NSA Spying." *Mother Jones,* June 27, 2013. https://www .motherjones.com/politics/2013/06/nsa-spying-occupy-homeland -security/.

Global Slavery Index. 2018. "Unravelling the Numbers." https://www .globalslaveryindex.org/2018/findings/highlights/.

Gorz, Andre. 1989. *Critique of Economic Reason.* Trans. Gillian Handyside and Chris Turner. London: Verso.

Gorz, Andre. 1999. *Reclaiming Work: Beyond the Wage-Based Society.* Trans. Chris Turner. Cambridge, UK: Polity Press.

Gramsci, Antonio. 1971. *Selections from the Prison Notebooks.* Trans. Quintin Hoare and Geoffrey N. Smith. New York: International Publishers.

Graeber, David. 2018. *Bullshit Jobs: A Theory*. New York: Simon and Schuster.

Guattari, Félix. 2008. *The Three Ecologies*. Trans. Paul Sutton and Ian Pindar. New York: Continuum.

Haider, Asad. 2018. *Mistaken Identity: Race and Class in the Age of Trump*. New York: Verso.

Hall, Derek. 2012. "Rethinking Primitive Accumulation: Theoretical Tensions and Rural Southeast Asian Complexities." *Antipode* 44, no. 4: 1188–208.

Hall, Stuart. 1986. "Gramsci's Relevance for the Study of Race and Ethnicity." *Journal of Communication Inquiry* 10, no. 2: 5–27.

Hallsworth, Simon, and John Lea. 2011. "Reconstructing Leviathan: Emerging Contours of the Security State." *Theoretical Criminology* 15, no. 2: 141–57.

Hardt, Michael, and Antonio Negri. 2009. *Commonwealth*. Cambridge, Mass.: Harvard University Press.

Hardt, Michael, and Antonio Negri. 2017. *Assembly*. New York: Oxford University Press.

Harvey, David. 2003. *The New Imperialism*. Oxford: Oxford University Press.

Harvey, David. 2005. *A Brief History of Neoliberalism*. Oxford: Oxford University Press.

Harvey, David. 2008. "The Right to the City." *New Left Review* 53 (September–October): 23–40.

Harvey, David. 2010. *A Companion to Marx's Capital*. London: Verso.

Harvey, D. 2014. *Seventeen Contradictions and the End of Capitalism*. London: Profile Books.

Hickel, J. 2015. "Could You Live On $1.90 a Day? That's the International Poverty Line." *The Guardian,* November 1, 2015. https://www.theguardian.com/global-development-professionals-network/2015/nov/01/global-poverty-is-worse-than-you-think-could-you-live-on-190-a-day.

Hitchen, E. 2016. "Living and Feeling the Austere." *New Formations* 87:102–18.

Hitchen, E., and Ian G. R. Shaw. 2019. "Intervention—Shrinking Worlds: Austerity and Depression." *Antipode* Online. https://antipodefoundation.org/2019/03/07/shrinking-worlds-austerity-and-depression/.

Holloway, J. 2002. "12 Theses on Changing the World without Taking Power." *The Commoner* 4. http://www.commoner.org.uk/04holloway2.pdf.

Hudson, Laura. 2011. "A Species of Thought: Bare Life and Animal Being." *Antipode* 43, no. 5: 1659–78.

International Labour Office. 2017. *World Employment and Social Outlook—Trends 2017*. Geneva.

The Invisible Committee. 2009. *The Invisible Committee: The Coming Insurrection*. Milton Keynes: Lightning Source.

Katz, Cindi. 2004. *Growing Up Global: Economic Restructuring and Children's Everyday Lives*. Minneapolis: University of Minnesota Press.

Khasnabish, Alex. 2017. "Cultivating the Radical Imagination in the North of the Americas." In *Why Don't the Poor Rise Up? Organizing the Twenty-First Century Resistance,* ed. Ajamu Nangwaya and Michael Truscello, 119–32. Chico, Calif.: AK Press.

Krugman, Paul. 2012. "Is Growth Over?" *The New York Times,* December 26, 2012. https://krugman.blogs.nytimes.com/2012/12/26/is-growth -over/.

Lapavitsas, Costas. 2013. *Profiting without Producing: How Finance Exploits Us All*. New York: Verso.

Laurie, Emma W., and Ian G. R. Shaw. 2018. "Violent Conditions: The Injustices of Being." *Political Geography* 65:8–16.

Lebaron, Genevieve, and Alison J. Ayers. 2013. "The Rise of a 'New Slavery'? Understanding African Unfree Labour through Neoliberalism." *Third World Quarterly* 34, no. 5: 873–92.

Lefebvre, Henri. 1991. *The Production of Space*. Trans. Donald Nicholson-Smith. Oxford, UK: Blackwell.

Lefebvre, Henri. 2009. *State, Space, World: Selected Essays*. Ed. Neil Brenner and Stuart Elden, trans. Gerald Moore, Neil Brenner, and Stuart Elden. Minneapolis: University of Minnesota Press.

Lenin V I. 1940 (1920). *Left-Wing Communism: An Infantile Disorder*. New York: International.

Li, Tania Murray. 2009. "To Make Live or Let Die? Rural Dispossession and the Protection of Surplus Populations." *Antipode* 41, no. 1: 66–93.

Lindell, Ilda. 2010. "Informality and Collective Organising: Identities, Alliances, and Transnational Activism in Africa." *Third World Quarterly* 31, no. 2: 207–22.

Linebaugh, Peter. 2014. *Stop, Thief! The Commons, Enclosures, and Resistance*. Oakland, Calif.: PM Press.

Luttrell, Johanna C. 2015. "Alienation and Global Poverty: Arendt on the Loss of the World." *Philosophy and Social Criticism* 41, no. 9: 869–84.

Manzo, Kate. 2005. "Modern Slavery, Global Capitalism, and Deproletarianisation in West Africa." *Review of African Political Economy* 32, no. 106: 521–34.

Marx, Karl. 1973. *Grundrisse*. Trans. Martin Nicolaus. London: Penguin Classics.

Marx, Karl. 1975. *Early Writings*. Trans. Rodney Livingstone and Gregor Benton. New York: Penguin.

Marx, Karl. 1988. *Economic and Philosophic Manuscripts of 1844*. Trans. Martin Milligan. New York: Prometheus Books.

Marx, Karl. 1990. *Capital: A Critique of Political Economy*. Trans. Ben Fowkes. London: Penguin Books.

Marx, Karl. 1999. *The Poverty of Philosophy*. Full text available at https://www.marxists.org/archive/marx/works/1847/poverty-philosophy/.

Marx, Karl. 2009. *The Class Struggles in France, 1848 to 1850*. Full text available at https://www.marxists.org/archive/marx/works/1850/class-struggles-france/.

Marx, Karl, and Fredrich Engels. 2015. *The Communist Manifesto*. Trans. Samuel Moore. Harmondsworth, UK: Penguin Classics.

Massey, Doreen. 2005. *For Space*. London: Sage Publications.

Mbembe, A. 2003. "Necropolitics." *Public Culture* 15, no. 1: 11–40.

McCarthy, James. 2005. "Commons as Counterhegemonic Projects." *Capitalism Nature Socialism* 16, no. 1: 9–24.

McIntyre, Michael, and Heidi J. Nast. 2011. "Bio(necro)polis: Marx, Surplus Populations, and the Spatial Dialectics of Reproduction and 'Race.'" *Antipode* 43, no. 5: 1465–88.

Merrifield, Andy. 2011. *Magical Marxism*. London: Pluto Press.

Merrifield, Andy. 2013, The Planetary Urbanization of Non-Work. *City* 17, no. 1: 20–36.

Mitchell, Katharyne. 2009. "Pre-black futures." *Antipode* 41, no. 1: 239–61.

Moises, Subcomandante. 2016. *Sixth Commission of the Zapatista Army for National Liberation. Critical Thoughts in the Face of the Capitalist Hydra I*. Durham, N.C.: Paperboat Press.

Monaghan, Angela. 2014. "US Wealth Inequality—Top 0.1% Worth as Much as the Bottom 90%." *The Guardian,* November 13, 2014. https://www.theguardian.com/business/2014/nov/13/us-wealth-inequality-top-01-worth-as-much-as-the-bottom-90.

Moore, Jason W. 2017. "The Capitalocene, Part I: On the Nature and Origins of Our Ecological Crisis." *Journal of Peasant Studies* 44, no. 3: 594–630.

Mora, Mariana. 2007. "Zapatista Anticapitalist Politics and the 'Other Campaign.'" *Latin American Perspectives* 34, no. 2: 64–77.

Mora, Mariana. 2015. "The Politics of Justice: Zapatista Autonomy at the Margins of the Neoliberal Mexican State." *Latin American and Caribbean Ethnic Studies* 10, no. 1: 87–106.

Munck, R. 2013. "The Precariat: A View from the South." *Third World Quarterly* 34, no. 5: 747–62.

Nancy, Jean-Luc. 2000. *Being Singular Plural*. Trans. Robert Richardson and Anne O'Byrne. Stanford, Calif.: Stanford University Press.

Nast, Heidi. 2015. "The Machine-Phallus: Psychoanalyzing the Geopolitical Economy of Masculinity and Race." *Psychoanalytic Inquiry* 35, no. 8: 766–85.

Nast, Heidi. 2017. "Queering the Maternal? Unhinging Supremacist Geographies of the Machine, Markets, and Recreational Pleasure." *Environment and Planning D: Society and Space Online*. October 31, 2017. https://societyandspace.org/2017/10/31/queering-the-maternal

-unhinging-supremacist-geographies-of-the-machine-markets-and
-recreational-pleasure/.

Neeson, Jeanette M. 1993. *Commoners: Common Right, Enclosure,
and Social Change in England, 1700–1820*. Cambridge: Cambridge
University Press.

Nevins, Joseph. 2017. "The Right to the World," *Antipode* 49, no. 5: 1349–
67.

Oxfam. 2017. *An Economy for the 99%*. Oxfam Briefing Papers, 210.

Pain, Rachel. 2015. "Intimate War." *Political Geography* 44:64–73.

Parenti, Christian. 2015. "The Environment Making State: Territory,
Nature, and Value." *Antipode* 47, no. 4: 829–48.

Piketty, Thomas. 2014. *Capital in the Twenty-First Century*. Trans. Arthur
Goldhammer. Cambridge, Mass.: Harvard University Press.

Polanyi, Karl. 2001. *The Great Transformation: The Political and Economic
Origins of Our Time*. Boston: Beacon Press.

Pratt, Geraldine. 2005. "Abandoned Women and Space of Exception."
Antipode 37, no. 5: 1052–78.

Pratt, Geraldine, Caleb Johnson, and Vanessa Banta. 2017. "Lifetimes of
Disposability and Surplus Entrepreneurs in Bagong Barrio, Manila."
Antipode 49, no. 1: 169–92.

Purcell, Mark. 2013. "Possible Worlds: Henri Lefebvre and the Right to the
City." *Journal of Urban Affairs* 36, no. 1: 141–54.

Roelvink, Gerda. 2016. *Building Dignified Worlds: Geographies of Collective
Action*. Minneapolis: University of Minnesota Press.

Robinson, C. J. 1983. *Black Marxism: The Making of the Black Radical
Tradition*. Chapel Hill: The University of North Carolina Press.

Prison Policy Initiative. 2018. *Mass Incarceration: The Whole Pie 2018*.
https://www.prisonpolicy.org/reports/pie2018.html.

Santos, Boaventura de Sousa. 2014. *Epistemologies of the South: Justice
against Epistemicide*. Abingdon, UK: Routledge.

Sassen, Saskia. 2014. *Expulsions: Brutality and Complexity in the Global
Economy*. Cambridge, Mass.: Harvard University Press.

Schindler, S. 2014. "The Making of 'World-Class' Delhi: Relations
between Street Hawkers and the New Middle Class." *Antipode* 46, no.
2: 557–73.

Sevilla-Buitrago, Alvaro. 2015. "Capitalist Formations of Enclosure: Space
and the Extinction of the Commons." *Antipode* 47, no. 4: 999–1020.

Shaw, Ian G. R. 2016. *Predator Empire: Drone Warfare and Full Spectrum
Dominance*. Minneapolis: The University of Minnesota Press.

Shaw, Ian G. R. 2017. "The Great War of Enclosure: Securing the Skies."
Antipode 4, 883–906.

Simone, AbdouMaliq. 2001. "Straddling the Divides: Remaking
Associational Life in the Informal African City." *International Journal
of Urban and Regional Planning* 25, no. 1: 102–17.

Simone, AbdouMaliq. 2013. "Cities of Uncertainty: Jakarta, the Urban Majority, and Inventive Political Technologies." *Theory, Culture & Society* 30, no. 7–8: 243–63.

Simone, AbdouMaliq. 2015. "The Urban Poor and Their Ambivalent Exceptionalities: Some Notes from Jakarta." *Current Anthropology* 56 (Supplement 11): S15–S23.

Simone, AbdouMaliq. 2016. "The Uninhabitable? In Between Collapsed Yet Still Rigid Distinctions." *Cultural Politics* 12, no. 2: 135–54.

Smith, Gavin A. 2011. "Selective Hegemony and Beyond-Populations with 'No Productive Function': A Framework for Enquiry." *Identities: Global Studies in Culture and Power* 18, no. 1: 2–38.

Soederberg, Susanne. 2013. "The US Debtfare State and the Credit Card Industry: Forging Spaces of Dispossession." *Antipode* 45, no. 2: 493–512.

Soja, Edward W. 2010. *Seeking Spatial Justice*. Minneapolis: University of Minnesota Press.

Springer, Simon. 2016. *The Anarchist Roots of Geography: Toward Spatial Emancipation*. Minneapolis: Minnesota University Press.

Statista. 2018. "Average Life Expectancy in Africa for Those Born in 2018, By Gender and Region (In Years)." https://www.statista.com/statistics /274511/life-expectancy-in-africa/.

Steel, G. 2012. "Whose Paradise? Itinerant Street Vendors' Individual and Collective Practices of Political Agency in the Tourist Streets of Cusco, Peru." *International Journal of Urban and Regional Research* 36, no. 5: 1007–21.

Streeck, Wolfgang. 2017. *How Will Capitalism End?* London: Verso.

Swyngedouw, Erik. 2009. "The Communist Hypothesis and Revolutionary Capitalisms: Exploring the Idea of Communist Geographies for the Twenty-first Century." *Antipode* 41, no. 1: 298–319.

Thompson, Edward P. 1963. *The Making of the English Working Class*. Harmondsworth, UK: Penguin Books.

UK Parliament. 2016. "Enclosing the Land." https://www.parliament.uk /about/living-heritage/transformingsociety/towncountry/landscape /overview/enclosingland/.

United Nations High Commissioner for Refugees. 2019. Figures at a Glance. https://www.unhcr.org/figures-at-a-glance.html.

Venn, Couze. 2018. *After Capital*. London: Sage.

Wacquant, Loïc. 2009. *Punishing the Poor: The Neoliberal Government of Social Insecurity*. Durham, N.C.: Duke University Press.

Wall, Tyler. 2016. "Ordinary Emergency: Drones, Police, and Geographies of Legal Terror." *Antipode* 48, no. 4: 1122–39.

Wallerstein, Immanuel. 2013. "Structural Crisis, or Why Capitalists May No Longer Find Capitalism Rewarding." In *Does Capitalism Have a Future?* ed. Immanuel Wallerstein, Randall Collins, Michael

Mann, Georgi Derluguian, and Craig Calhoun, 9–36. Oxford: Oxford University Press.

Ward, Callum, and Erik Swyngedouw. 2018. "Neoliberalisation from the Ground Up: Insurgent Capital, Regional Struggle, and the Assetisation of Land," *Antipode* 50, no. 4: 1077–97.

Waterstone, M. 2010. "Smoke and Mirrors: Inverting the Discourse on Tobacco." *Antipode* 42, no. 4: 875–96.

Watts, Michael J. 2011. "Planet of the Wageless." *Identities: Global Studies in Culture and Power* 18, no. 1: 69–80.

Wright, M. W. 2011. "Necropolitics, Narcopolitics, and Femicide: Gendered Violence on the Mexico–U.S. Border." *Signs: Journal of Women in Culture and Society* 36, no. 3: 707–31.

Whitson, Risa. 2011. "Negotiating Place and Value: Geographies of Waste and Scavenging in Buenos Aires." *Antipode* 43. no. 4: 1404–33.

World Health Organization 2017. "Depression: Let's Talk." http://www .who.int/mental_health/management/depression/en/.

Žižek, Slavoj. 1989. *The Sublime Object of Ideology*. London: Verso.

(Continued from page iii)

Shannon Mattern
Deep Mapping the Media City

Steven Shaviro
No Speed Limit: Three Essays on Accelerationism

Jussi Parikka
The Anthrobscene

Reinhold Martin
Mediators: Aesthetics, Politics, and the City

John Hartigan Jr.
Aesop's Anthropology: A Multispecies Approach

Ian Shaw is senior lecturer in human geography in the School of Geographical and Earth Sciences at the University of Glasgow. He is author of *Predator Empire* (Minnesota, 2016).

Marv Waterstone is professor emeritus in the School of Geography and Development at the University of Arizona, where he has been a faculty member for more than thirty years. He currently coteaches a course each spring titled "What Is Politics?" with professor Noam Chomsky.